MAKING WOOD BOXES WITH A BAND SAW

MAKING WOOD BOXES WITH A BAND SAW

Tom Crabb

Sterling Publishing Co., Inc.   New York

Edited and designed by Robert Hernandez

Library of Congress Cataloging in Publication Data

Crabb, Tom.
    Making wood boxes with a band saw.

    Includes index.
    1. Woodwork. 2. Boxes, Wooden. I. Title.
TT200.C73 1985   745.593   85-8068
ISBN 0-8069-6246-1 (pbk.)

Second Printing, 1986

Copyright © 1985 by Tom Crabb
Published by Sterling Publishing Co., Inc.
Two Park Avenue, New York, N.Y. 10016
Distributed in Australia by Capricorn Book Co. Pty. Ltd.
Unit 5C1 Lincoln St., Lane Cove, N.S.W. 2066
Distributed in the United Kingdom by Blandford Press
Link House, West Street, Poole, Dorset BH15 1LL, England
Distributed in Canada by Oak Tree Press Ltd.
% Canadian Manda Group, P.O. Box 920, Station U
Toronto, Ontario, Canada M8Z 5P9
Manufactured in the United States of America

Contents

To Angela
For all the right reasons

Introduction

Wood has more uses than any other material on earth. We use it for generating heat, making houses, and creating art, and we have been using it far longer than any other material. Wood has a magical quality that attracts us to it, and it remains the most prized and workable material at hand. And it's everywhere. Wood grows like magic all by itself.

Of all the wood on earth, no two scraps are ever the same. You cannot make exact duplicates of anything in wood. Size, shape, and function can be the same, but the figure in the grain is always different. This is the magic of wood.

Many of the boxes in this book are made from two 2 by 4s or 2 by 6s glued together, which yield blocks that are 3 by 3½ inches or 3 by 5½ inches, respectively. Most of the wood is yellow pine, poplar, some fir and cedar. There is an occasional piece of semiexotic wood, and, of course, we shouldn't forget plywood.

Mostly, band-saw boxes are made out of wood scraps or parts of trees, or wood that someone donates to you. Wood is not hard to come by in small pieces. You can find scraps of 2 by 4s at most construction sites. Take them home and save them.

In short, if you can saw it and sand it, you can make a band-saw box out of it.

Illus. 1. The Black & Decker 7½-inch band saw, powered by a ⅜-inch electric drill, is inexpensive and can fit in the smallest of workshops.

The Band Saw

The band saw is a unique tool because it has only a cutting stroke. You never have to draw the blade back through the wood after making a cut. This is the only saw that works that way, and it is the most efficient cutting tool yet devised. You might think a circular saw has only a cutting stroke, but the back of the blade must come up through the wood in order to get the teeth up front to cut. The band saw is such a good idea I wish I had thought of it. But, I wish I had thought of the wheel, too.

Another unique aspect about the band saw is that the blade is very thin because it only goes in one direction. Since it is so narrow, the *kerf* (the slit or groove made in the wood by the sawing action) is also thin, which is necessary for making band-saw boxes. If you saw a piece of wood in two in any direction and carefully glue the pieces back together, you will have to look very closely to see any disturbance in the figure of the wood. With this unique ability of the band saw you can dissect a piece of wood and glue it back together leaving out selected inside portions.

Band saws come in a wide variety of sizes. Many of the boxes in this book were made on the smallest band saw I know of, the Black & Decker 7½-inch band saw powered by a ⅜-inch electric drill. This saw (Illus. 1) will yield satisfactory results for the weekend woodworker. It is inexpensive (under $80), and the electric drill is easily removed for other uses. This band saw is particularly good for people who work in small spaces. Other boxes were made on a Craftsman 12-inch band saw with a ½-horsepower motor. Both saws do the job.

As with any tool, the band saw should be kept clean and in good condition: the blade guides adjusted, the table kept at 90 degrees to the blade, the weld on the blade inspected and the right tension maintained. All of these things should be checked periodically to make sure you get accurate saw cuts.

Here are a couple of don'ts which I feel obligated to mention about the band saw:

Don't strain the motor either by feeding the wood too fast or by trying to turn a corner too short for the blade you are using.

Don't make any adjustments to the saw while it's running. Turn the saw off before backing the blade out.

And the biggest don't of all: *Don't* put your fingers in the path of the blade.

Most band-saw manufacturers provide a large selection of blades for their saws, but I use only two for making band-saw boxes. A ¼-inch 14- or 15-tooth blade is used most of the time because it can take a lot of tension and it saws straight. However, it

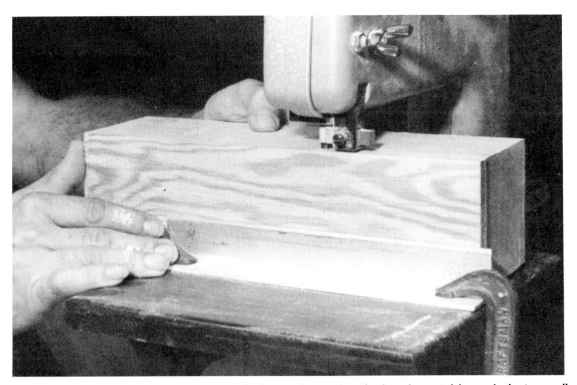

Illus. 2. A homemade rip fence clamped to the band-saw table works just as well as a store-bought one. The one in the illustration is a piece of 1½-inch-by-1½-inch aluminum angle.

Illus. 3. A store-bought rip fence in use.

will only turn a ¾-inch radius, which for most boxes in this book is all you need. A ⅛-inch 14- or 15-tooth blade is also handy because it will turn a ¼-inch radius. A ⅛-inch blade will also saw straight, but you must feed the wood to the saw more slowly. If you are approaching a knot or a sudden change in the direction of the grain, you need to go even more slowly.

One extra item you will need for your band saw is a *rip fence*. This can simply be two pieces of wood the same length as your band-saw table, glued and screwed together at the edge to form a right angle, which you can clamp to the table parallel to the blade. A length of aluminum angle or angle iron works just as well (Illus. 2). I use a store-bought rip fence made to fit my band saw (Illus. 3). It isn't any better than the ones described above—it's just more convenient.

To use the rip fence, measure the distance you want from the blade, square the fence from the edge of the table with an adjustable square, and clamp the fence to the table. You can now cut a straight block of wood using the fence as a guide.

Construction Tips

The making of a band-saw box is unique among woodworking techniques because you begin with a solid piece of wood that you saw apart and then put back together. Since each piece sawn off is glued back in its original position there is no fussing to fit pieces together or to achieve tight-fitting joints. This allows a continuity of grain inside and out which adds to the uniqueness of each box. As a result, each band-saw box is different by both design and the grain of the wood.

Band-saw boxes are made with two basic techniques, each of which allows for a variety of design possibilities. One technique is to saw ¼ inch off the back of the block of wood using the rip fence (Illus. 4). On the front of the block, outline the drawer shapes so they can be cut out with one continuous saw cut. This usually is a figure-8 shape. (Variations on this theme are given in the instructions for each box.) Enter the block of wood either at the top or bottom of the wood and exit through the same saw kerf. Remove the cutout drawer blocks and glue the back piece to its original position (Illus. 5). Glue a ¹⁄₁₆-inch spline in to fill the saw kerf at the entrance, if it is necessary. Any shaping that is to be done to the outside of the box is now possible.

The drawers of this type of box are

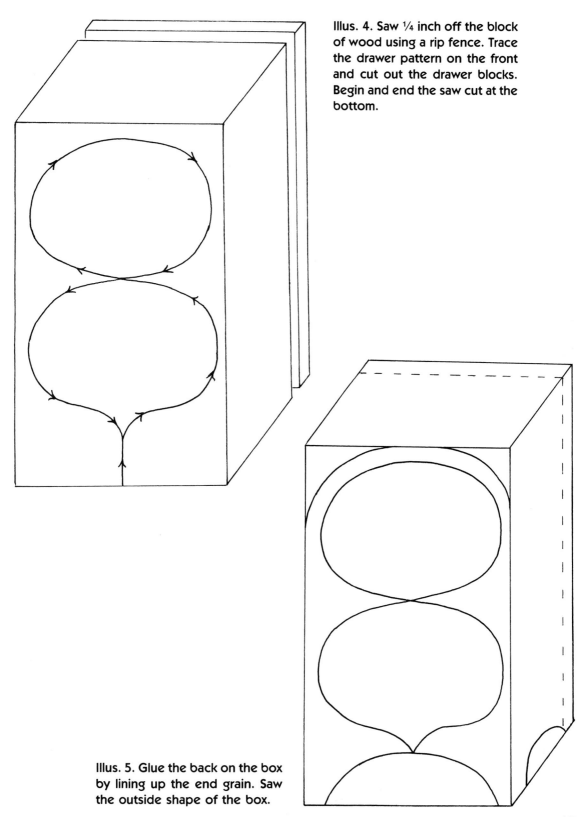

Illus. 4. Saw ¼ inch off the block of wood using a rip fence. Trace the drawer pattern on the front and cut out the drawer blocks. Begin and end the saw cut at the bottom.

Illus. 5. Glue the back on the box by lining up the end grain. Saw the outside shape of the box.

made by sawing ³⁄₁₆–¼ inch off the front and back of the drawer block using the rip fence. The shape of the drawer space is then drawn on the front and cut out. Now glue the back and front of the drawer into place, making sure to line up the grain pattern (Illus. 6). Most boxes of this type look best if the drawer edges and the corresponding edges of the box are sanded to a smooth, round edge.

The second type of box gives a more studied appearance with square-cornered drawers and straight lines. Begin by sawing ¼ inch off each side of the block of wood (Illus. 7). Then lay the block on its side and draw the shape of the drawer blocks on it. Each drawer must be cut out as one piece, which means a radius must be turned with the saw blade on one back corner of each drawer block. I usually put the radius corner on the bottom. After the drawer blocks are removed the sides can be glued back on the box (Illus. 8).

While the glue is drying on the box, the drawers can be made (Illus. 9). Saw ³⁄₁₆–¼ inch off both sides of the drawer blocks using a rip fence. On the side of the drawer block, draw the shape of the inside space. With the drawer space cut out, glue the sides back on, sand them, and add drawer pulls.

For this type of box it sometimes is a good idea to put the drawers in place and give the front a good sanding with the belt sander. This frequently gets everything settled at the same level.

When gluing the box and drawers

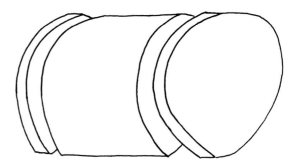

Illus. 6a. Cut ¼ inch off the front and back of the drawer block using a rip fence.

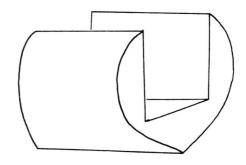

Illus. 6b. Trace the drawer space on the front of the drawer block and cut it out.

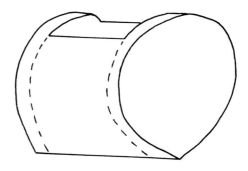

Illus. 6c. Glue the front and back on the drawer.

back together, be sure to match the end grain to make sure each piece is in its correct position.

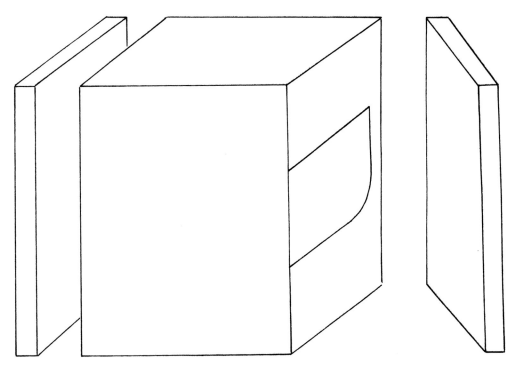

Illus. 7. Saw ¼ inch off each side of the block using a rip fence.

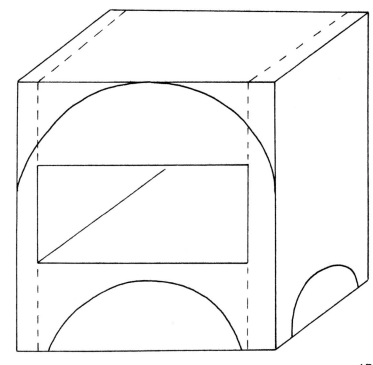

Illus. 8. Glue the sides back on the box by lining up the end grain. Saw the outside shape of the box.

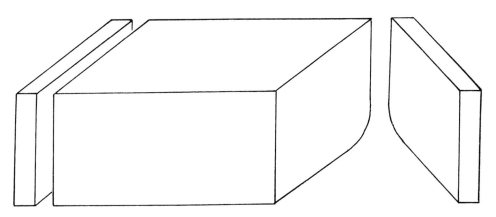

Illus. 9a. Saw ¼ inch off each side of the drawer block.

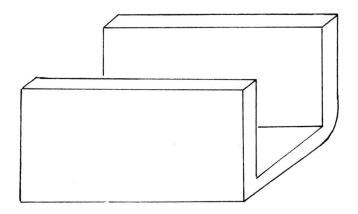

Illus. 9b. Trace the drawer space on the side of the drawer block and cut it out.

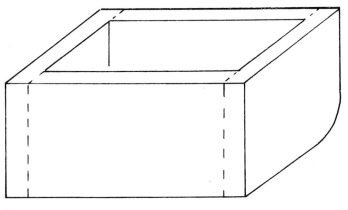

Illus. 9c. Glue the sides back on the drawer by lining up the end grain.

SCALING UP

Most of the drawings in this book are made on ½-inch squares. If a drawing needs to be scaled up to something other than the usual ½-inch squares, then the instructions will say so. (See Illus. 10 for scaling up to ¾-inch squares.)

The real difficulty in scaling things up is drawing all those little squares, but you don't have to do it every time. Take a piece of white poster board, about 11 by 14 inches, and draw ¾-inch squares all over it with a fine black soft-tip pen. When you want to scale up a drawing lay a sheet of paper over the poster board and tape it down at the corners. You can see the little squares right through most paper. When the drawing is finished unfasten the corners carefully and put away the poster board for another use.

The best way to do the actual drawing is to make a short mark everywhere a line from the. drawing crosses a line of a square. After all the lines have been marked, all that's left to do is fill in the blanks.

GLUING AND CLAMPING

Gluing and clamping are important steps for making band-saw boxes. You must make sure the grain is matched on the pieces being glued and that they stay matched as pressure is applied by the clamp. The glue between the two pieces of wood will act as a lubricant, so if the clamp is not exactly square to the surface one of the parts will slide out of line. You will have to ease off the clamp, re-

align the grain, and clamp again. The one thing you can do to keep this nuisance to a minimum is to not overload the joint with glue. A very thin layer is quite enough.

When choosing a glue, you can use most any sticky kind that dries hard. My preference is Titebond. It comes in a handy applicator bottle for squeezing out small amounts, it bonds and dries quickly, helping to prevent the dreaded clamp-induced slide. Clamping time is usually about an hour.

I also keep a little epoxy around, the kind that comes in a double syringe. It is used mostly for gluing drawer pulls because epoxy needs only contact to work. I also use it as a filler. If there is a check or a void of any sort on the outside surface of a piece of wood you want to use, mix a little epoxy with some sawdust and push it into the hole. This does not make the check disappear; it only fills it and makes the wood stronger.

Clamping pressure is important to the glue and to achieve as thin a glue line as possible. Manufacturers generally recommend a glue line of .002 inches and 2000 lbs. of pressure per square inch. That's all very interesting but not very practical. Basically, here's what you do: use as many clamps as you can get on the box, use clamp pads to spread the pressure, and tighten them as much as you can without crushing the box.

SANDING

All boxes require the same amount of sanding. That is, simply, sand till

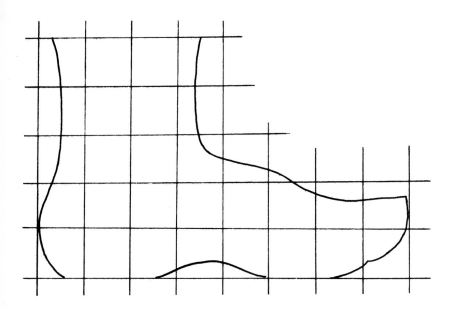

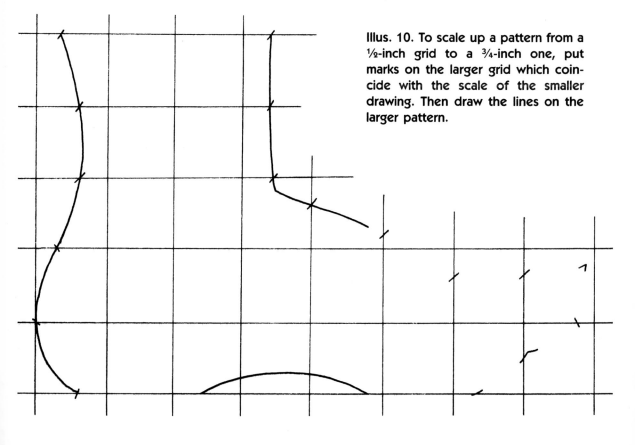

Illus. 10. To scale up a pattern from a ½-inch grid to a ¾-inch one, put marks on the larger grid which coincide with the scale of the smaller drawing. Then draw the lines on the larger pattern.

they are smooth. Boxes with flat sides can be sanded with power tools. A belt sander is the fastest and most versatile of them all, and it can be clamped to a bench or sawhorse as you hold the box to the sander (Illus. 11). This arrangement will accomplish 80 percent of the required sanding.

For the other 20 percent, there are many types of sanding devices that fit into an electric drill: drum sanders (Illus. 12), little clip-on disc sanders (Illus. 13), and mini-strippers, which are devices that have strips of sandpaper coming out from a central hub (Illus. 14). One word of caution about the mini-stripper: when using the coarse grit on softwood, it tends to beat out the soft part of the grain and leave the hard part sticking up so the wood feels lumpy. The fine-grit mini-stripper, however, will polish the wood to a fine lustre, especially if you have a light touch. All these sanding devices for the electric drill work best, generally speaking, if the drill is mounted to a bench and the box is held in your hand.

Finally, we come to the stage of sanding by hand. If you have been able to sand the surface down with a machine, then you can probably start sanding with 150-grit paper and then go to 220-grit. If you have not been able to sand the surface at all, it's best to start with 60-grit paper, progressing to 80, 100, 150, and finally 220.

Sanding makes scratches in the wood; the smaller the scratches the

Illus. 11. Two useful sanding arrangements: an electric drill and belt sander clamped to a sawhorse.

Illus. 12. Drum sanders of assorted sizes are a great help for shaping edges and rounding corners.

Illus. 13. Disc sanders for an electric drill are useful and come in different sizes.

Illus. 14. Mini-strippers of various sizes in fine grits are good for sanding curved surfaces.

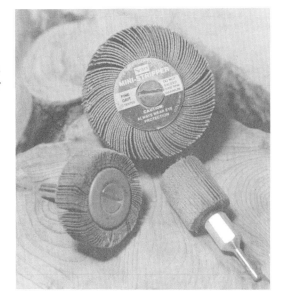

better the wood looks. If you started hand-sanding a rough piece of wood with 220-grit paper, you would never get it smooth. The idea is to start with a coarse sandpaper and work your way up to a fine grade. It goes faster than you might think. Sanding with the grain of the wood helps hide the scratches.

When you are ready for the 220-grit sanding take a damp cloth and wipe the surface of the box and let it dry. This will raise the grain a little and stiffen the little wood fibres that stick up like tiny hairs. When you sand the box with the 220-grit paper it will cut off the hairs and smooth the grain to a near-gloss.

FINISHING

Finishing is the fun part because it is the last stage in making your bandsaw box. But there are always questions about the type of finish to use. You can use light or dark stain, oil, wax, or varnish.

Every piece of wood has two main parts, the early wood and the late wood. With softwoods (pine, fir, cedar), the early wood is the lighter, soft part of the grain, which absorbs a lot of stain, and the late wood is the darker, hard part, which soaks up very little. In effect, the figure (grain pattern) of the wood has been visually diminished. Pine is never going to look like walnut, anyway.

With hardwoods the story is a little different. The early wood is the darker part, which soaks up stain making it darker than the late wood, which is lighter, so the contrast in the figure is heightened. I do not often stain hardwoods. The one use I make of stain is to create contrast within the box itself. Staining the box one tone and the drawers another can separate one part visually from another.

All wood needs a finish to seal it. The finish I use almost to the exclusion of others is varnish. Polyurethane varnish in spray cans is a great convenience to woodworkers. Just set your box on a piece of scrap wood and spray it a couple of times. When the varnish is hard I usually take a small pad of 0000 steel wool, dip it in linseed oil, rub down the whole box and wipe off the excess oil. This takes out any little dust particles that settled in the varnish and adds a very light sheen, leaving the surface smooth and soft to the touch.

Gnome Homes

Gnome-home boxes are the backbone of the band-saw-box fleet. Everyone likes them, they are quick and easy to make, they scale up or down without any difficulty, and they are the basis for some of the more elaborate boxes later in the book.

This particular box is 3¾ × 3¾ × 12½ inches and is made of poplar. You can build it with two 2 by 4s or a piece of 4 by 4. The design here should be scaled up to ¾-inch squares (Illus. 16 contains ½-inch squares).

Trace the pattern on the front of the block and saw ¼ inch off the back using the rip fence. Cut out the drawer blocks with one continuous cut starting at the bottom and making figure-8s until you reach the starting position. Then turn the saw off and back the blade out the entrance kerf. At this point you have two choices. One is to cut a ¹⁄₁₆-inch spline and glue it into the entrance kerf to hide it. Or you can take a knife and round the edges of the kerf and sand them smooth so they become part of the design of the box. Then glue the kerf and clamp it shut. With that done, glue the back on the block and cut out the outside shape.

Saw ¼ inch off the front and back of the drawer blocks and cut out the inside space, then glue the front and back on the drawers. Sand everything well, add drawer pulls, spray with varnish, then rub with linseed oil and 0000 steel wool.

This box can be made with one, two, three, or four drawers, depending on the length of wood you use.

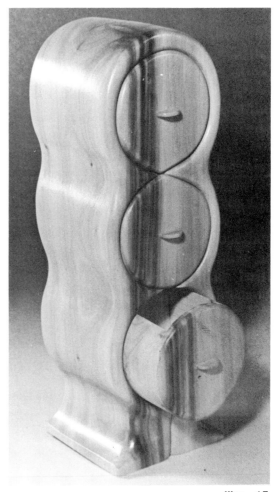

Illus. 15

24

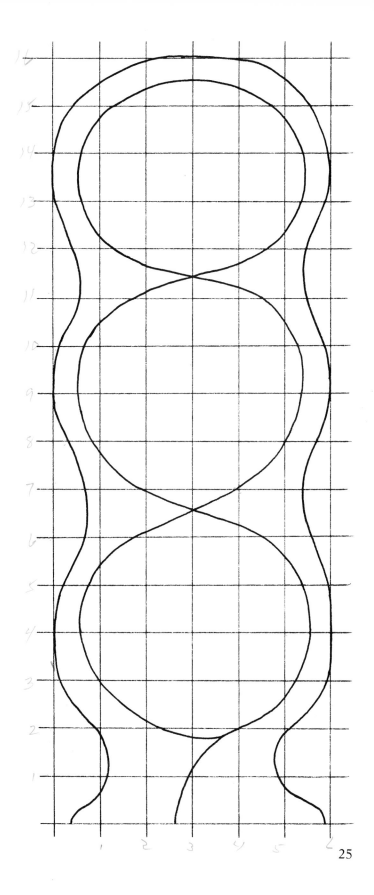

Illus. 16. Scale up the pattern on ¾-inch squares. Cut out the drawer spaces after making an entry cut at the bottom.

25

Plywood Box

Whenever you build something with plywood there are leftover scraps. Well, here's a good way to make use of plywood scraps. Glue them together and make band-saw boxes.

This box is four pieces of $\frac{3}{4}$- × 3- × $8\frac{3}{4}$-inch plywood glued together. The plywood doesn't have to be $\frac{3}{4}$ inch; you can glue $\frac{1}{2}$ inch or even mix different thicknesses of plywood. The box can also be made shorter or taller by removing or adding a drawer. It can be a case of making the box fit the material at hand.

Draw the pattern on the face of the plywood block (Illus. 18), then saw off both sides along the inside wavy line. Mark the drawer blocks on the side and cut them out. Glue the sides back on the box. Saw $\frac{1}{4}$ inch off each side of the three drawer blocks, cut out the inside drawer spaces, then glue the sides back on the drawers. Now saw the outside shape of the box. Sand everything, add drawer pulls, and finish as you wish.

Stain the box with Min-Wax Puritan Pine stain, then spray with varnish.

One of the unfortunate things about plywood is that the glue which holds the veneers together is so hard and brittle that it will take the fine cutting edge off a new blade in short order. If I plan to make a plywood box, I wait until the blade is just about ready to be replaced. After I make the plywood box I put a new blade on the band saw.

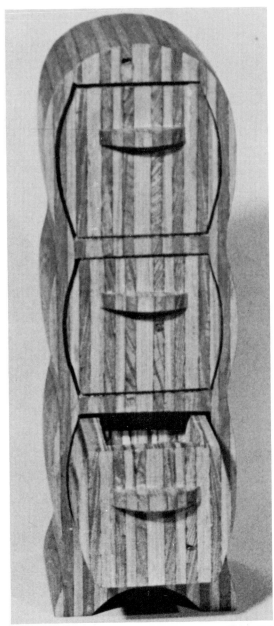

Illus. 17

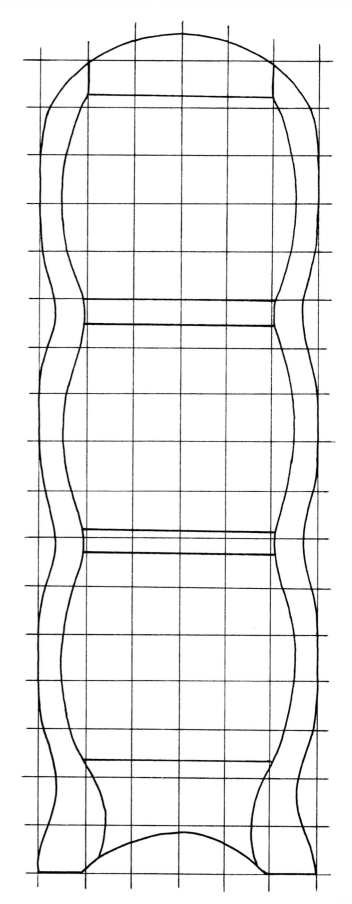

Illus. 18. First saw off both sides of the box, cutting along the inside wavy lines.

Stack-and-Swivel Box

Since nice boxes are made with plywood, here's another one. All of those thin layers of wood glued to-

gether create a striking visual effect. Many of the other boxes in this book can be made with plywood if you wish. This particular box makes use of the fact that plywood comes in dif-

ferent thicknesses. The basic block is made of four pieces of ¾-inch plywood, yielding a 3-inch cube when glued together. Three cubes stacked together are 9 inches tall. Cut out the drawer blocks without sawing ¼ inch off the sides (Illus. 20a). After the drawer blocks are cut out, glue the sides on the box using pieces of ¼-inch plywood.

Then cut ¼ inch off each side of the drawer blocks, cut out the inside spaces, and glue the sides back on. The drawer pulls are half of a 1½-inch-diameter circle cut from a 3/16-inch stack of plywood cut across the grain.

Attach the three boxes together with two ¼-inch dowels, which fit into ¼-inch holes in the boxes. Drill the holes ⅝ inch from the side and back, all the way into the box, but stop the dowel just short of the inside so it won't interfere with the drawer.

Drill the hole for the top box in the bottom back right corner; drill the middle box in its top and bottom back left corners; drill the bottom box in its top back right corner (Illus. 20b). Don't glue anything or the swivel is lost.

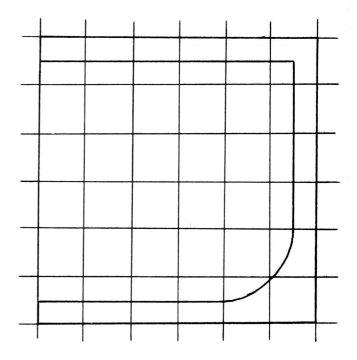

Illus. 20a. The basic unit of the stack-and-swivel box, as seen from the side.

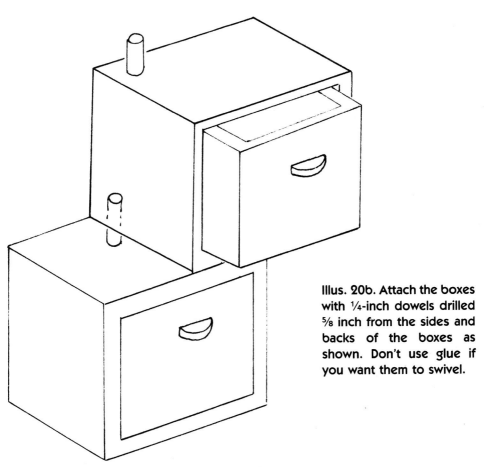

Illus. 20b. Attach the boxes with ¼-inch dowels drilled ⅝ inch from the sides and backs of the boxes as shown. Don't use glue if you want them to swivel.

Domino Box

The name of this box indicates that it was designed to hold a set of double-six dominoes. It was. One drawer was for dominoes, the other for a pad and pencil. I probably shouldn't admit this, but I made the domino drawer 1/16 inch too small. It's still a nice box with a contemporary look even though it won't hold a full set of dominoes. For sentimental reasons, I still call it the domino box.

It's made from a single piece of 7⅜- × 4¾- × 3-inch poplar. This means it could just as easily be made from two 2 by 6s glued together. The dimensions can change to fit whatever need you have for the box.

The tricky thing about this box is that to get to the drawer blocks you must saw ¼ inch off the end grain. These two pieces are weak and will probably break if you drop them. Cut out the drawers by standing the block on end and cutting the deep dimension through the wood (Illus. 22). The cut is not hard to do, but keeping the block perpendicular on the table takes some care. After the drawer blocks are cut out the main housing is fragile, so don't drop it, either.

After you glue the ends back, the box is structurally stable again. Glue it with care to make sure everything lines up—especially the middle shelf on which the top drawer slides.

All the above warnings apply to the drawers as well. They can easily break before the ends are glued back in place.

Finish the box with varnish and linseed oil rubbed into it with 0000 steel wool.

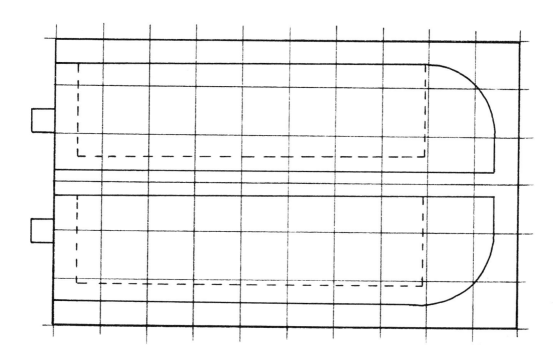

Illus. 22. A side view of the domino box. Cut out the drawer spaces as indicated by the dotted lines.

Pyramid Box

This box has one drawer on each of its four sides. It is made from a 9¾- × 3½- × 3½-inch piece of oak.

The outside shapes of most band-saw boxes are made after the drawer blocks have been removed and the boxes glued back together. That doesn't work with this box because the sides of the drawers must taper with the sides of the box (Illus. 24a and b). First saw the block of wood to the taper shown, then saw ¼ inch off the opposite sides.

Cut out the first two drawer blocks as indicated, making sure they pull out from opposite directions. To cut out the drawers, adjust the band-saw table to a 5-degree angle of taper. This is to make the top and bottom of the drawer faces horizontal. Cutting out the drawer blocks at an angle will make them look odd at the back. Regardless, they still work and can't be seen unless the drawer is pulled out all the way.

After the first two drawer blocks are cut out (actually the bottom and third drawers), glue the sides on the block. Now square the table and make the first two drawers. After the glue is dry, saw ¼ inch off the other two sides that were not sawn off before. Reset the angle on the table and cut out the remaining two drawer blocks. Then glue the sides back in

place on the box. Be sure when gluing that the drawer spaces already cut match up with the spaces in the box.

Square the saw table again and make the last two drawers. After the glue has set, fit the drawers in the box and sand with a belt or pad sander. Do this with the drawers in place since it makes them all come out

Illus. 23

32

flush. Add drawer pulls—cutoff heads of clothespins—and sand a ¼-inch chamfer on the four corners and around the top by holding the box about 45 degrees to a belt sander clamped to the workbench. Finish to your preference.

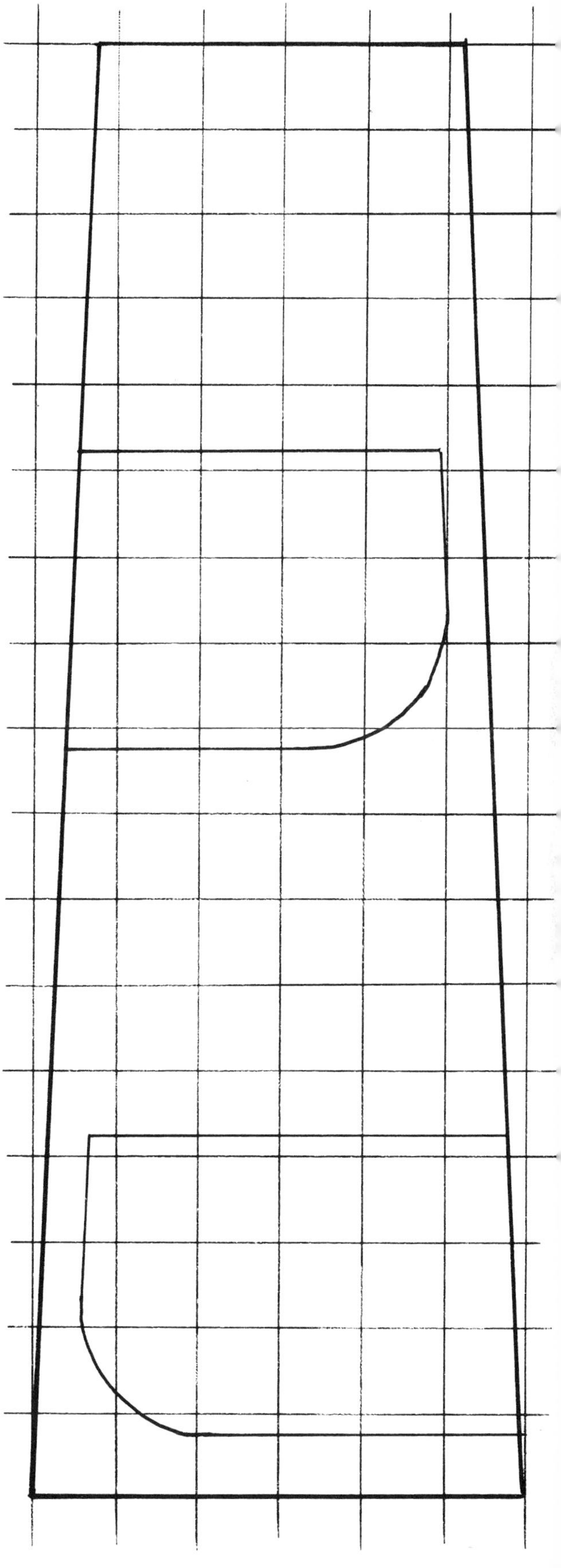

Illus. 24a. The pattern for sides one and three of the pyramid box. To cut out the drawer, adjust the band-saw table at a 5-degree angle. See Illus. 24b on the next page for the pattern for the other two sides.

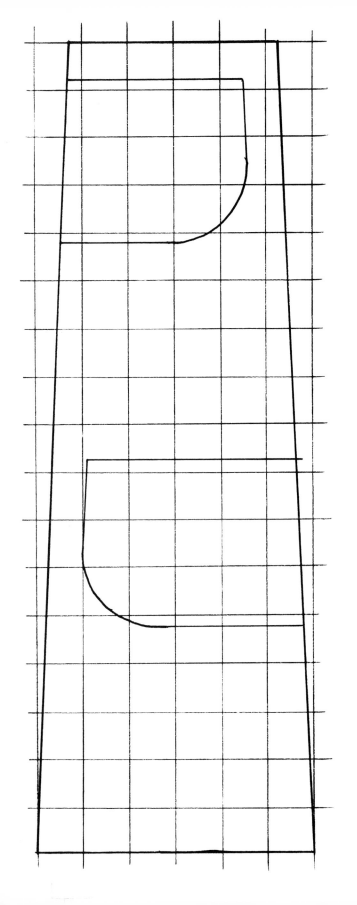

Illus. 24b. The pattern for sides two and four.

Loose-Lid Boxes

Loose-lid boxes are quick and easy to make. The shape and scale can be changed to suit your needs. This box is especially suitable as a very small and delicate box.

Make the larger box from two 7-inch-long pieces of 2 by 4 glued together (Illus. 26a). Saw off a ¼-inch piece from each side, then cut out the lid and inside space. Glue the sides back in place and shape the outside profile. Fit the lid to the box and glue a lid pull to the top, which can be anything large enough to pick up with your fingers. Then sand and finish the whole box. It's a fast job.

The smaller box is a good example of how to take a simple procedure and make it complicated. Make this box from three unmarred pieces of 1- × 2½- × 5-inch-long wood (Illus. 26b). Glue them together with a layer of dark veneer between each piece. That's the first complication, but it isn't a hard one.

The next complication is that the box is lined—in this case with velour. It could also be lined with the same veneer used between the layers. After all the parts of the box have been cut out—the sides, the lid, and the inside space—cut a piece of material which will cover the ends and the bottom of the box. In this case it will be 8 inches long and 2 inches wide (leave yourself a little extra width). Cut out two

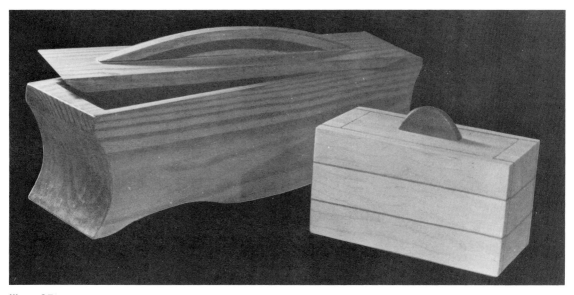

Illus. 25

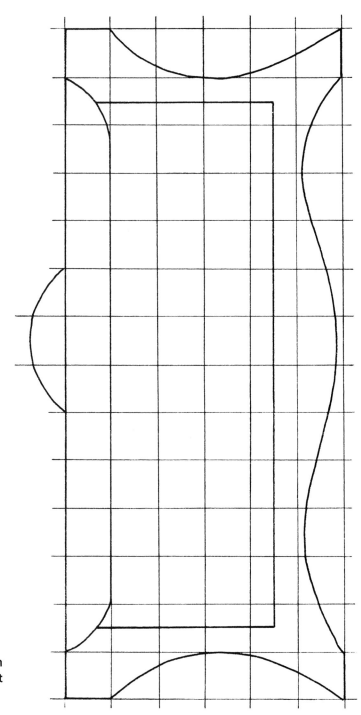

Illus. 26a. First saw off a ¼-inch piece from each side. Then cut out the lid and inside space.

pieces which will cover the sides of the box (5 by 2½ inches). Using contact cement as directed on the bottle, glue the material in the appropriate places. Now trim off any excess material with a sharp knife or razor blade and glue the box together with wood glue and clamp up firmly. After the glue is dry, sand and finish the box as you wish.

A lining can be used on any drawer-type box. Once the drawer has been lined the sides of the drawer will have to be sanded down a little in order to compensate for the thickness of the liner.

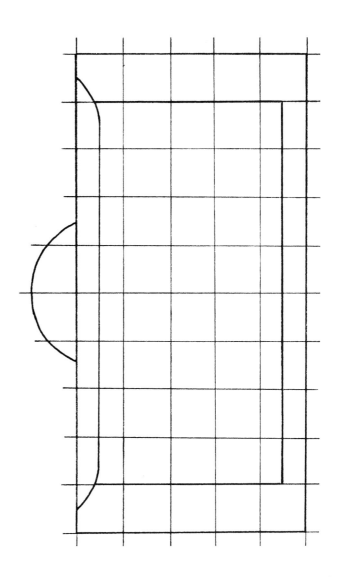

Illus. 26b. Glue three pieces of wood together with a darker veneer between each piece. Cut out according to the instructions for Illus. 26a.

Flip-Top Boxes

Illus. 27. The one-lid box is on the left; the two-lid box at right.

When you turn the knobs on these boxes the tops flip up. These boxes can be made in a wide variety of shapes and sizes with one or two lids. Not only can you scale these boxes up or down but the proportion can be changed to suit whatever need you might have.

The lids hinge on ¼-inch dowels cut an inch longer than the box is wide. The knobs on the two-lid box are wooden beads from a craft shop. Drill ¼-inch-diameter holes in the beads and glue them onto the ends of the ¼-inch dowels.

Make the two-lid box from a single piece of 2- × 4- × 7½-inch-long fir (Illus. 28a). Locate and drill the ¼-inch holes for the dowels first, then saw ¼ inch off each side of the 2 by 4.

Lay out the pattern for the lids and the inside space on the remaining block, cut them out, and glue the sides back in place leaving off the lids.

After the glue is dry, sand all the sides of the box except the top, which you sand after the lids have been fitted. A little sanding is required on the edges of the lids and the hole for the dowel in the sides of the box. The dowel should turn easily through the sides of the box but not in the lid. When the box is assembled and ready to finish, drill a ¹⁄₁₆-inch hole from inside the lid of the box into the dowel, dab a little glue on a round toothpick, insert it into the hole, then break off the toothpick. This is to make sure the dowel does not slip inside the lid.

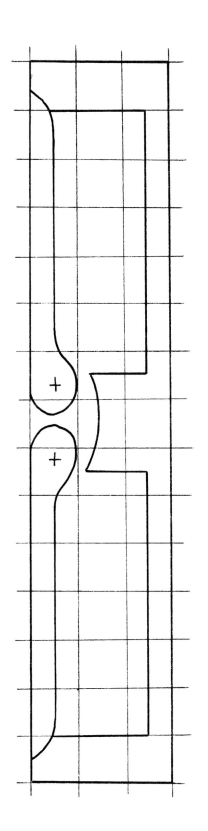

The second box requires essentially the same procedure (Illus. 28b). Drill the dowel hole for the hinge. Saw ¼ inch off the sides. Cut out the lid and the inside space. Glue the sides back in place and fit the lid.

Illus. 28a. (left) Drill ¼-inch holes for the dowels, indicated by the crosses.

Illus. 28b. (below) Follow the same instructions for the one-lid box.

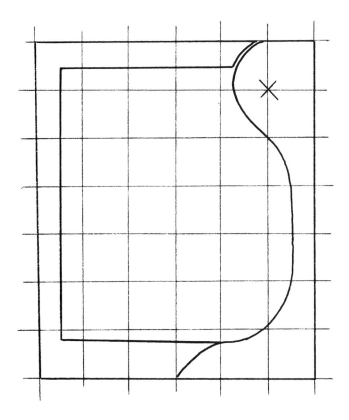

Bin Box

This is a nifty little box. Actually, you can make it as big as you wish. I'll probably make a bigger one the next chance I get. It is basically a flip-top type of box that opens forward from the side.

Make the box from three pieces of 1 by 4 white pine laminated together. The overall size of the block is $2\frac{1}{2} \times 2\frac{1}{4} \times 5\frac{1}{2}$ inches. First drill a $\frac{1}{8}$-inch hole, located as indicated in the drawing by the cross (Illus. 30a), all the way through the side of the block. This is the point at which the bin hinges. Next saw $\frac{3}{16}-\frac{1}{4}$ inch off both sides of the block using the rip fence. Now cut out the bin block in one long cut starting at the top of the bin. After the bin block is out, glue the sides back on the box.

Saw $\frac{3}{16}$ inch off both sides of the bin block, then cut out the space indicated by the dotted line in the drawing. Glue the sides back in place. After the glue dries, sand the sides of the bin a little so the bin will swing out with ease. Don't forget to round the lower front corner of the bin or it will not swing out at all.

Fit the bin in the box and position it with a $\frac{1}{8}$-inch length of dowel. With the bin in place, sand the box on all sides before adding the drawer pull, which is a two-inch piece of $\frac{1}{4}$-inch dowel glued $\frac{3}{4}$ inch below the top.

Now the bin box is ready for wood stain and finish of your choice.

Illus. 29

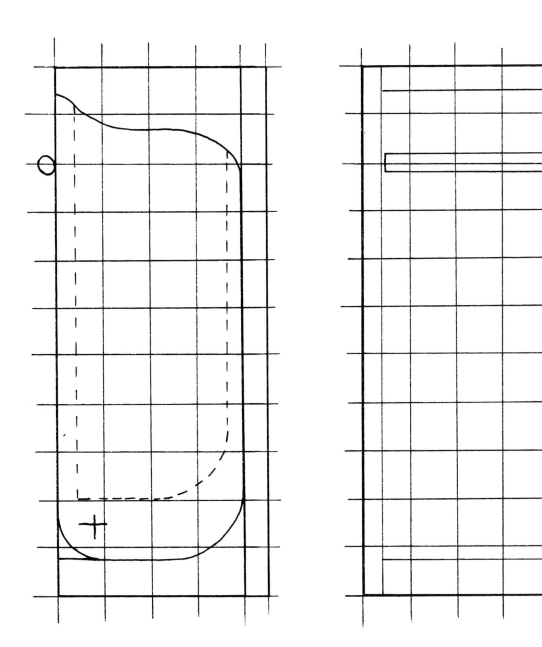

Illus. 30a. Drill a ⅛-inch hole, indicated by the cross at bottom. Cut out the inside space, indicated by the dotted line.

Illus. 30b. The front view of the bin box.

Hinged-Lid Box #1

Illus. 31

Hinged-lid boxes are generally quick to make until you get to the hinge part, which requires a little time. The small brass hinges (⅝ by ¾ inch) can be purchased in most hardware stores at four in a package for a couple of dollars. They have to be put in flush and squarely so the lid will close properly. Since the space and the amount of wood you are working with is very small, the best tool to use for this job is a sharp knife.

This particular box is made with three pieces of 1-by-7 white pine laminated together (Illus. 32). The dimensions and proportions are not critical and can be changed to suit your needs.

First cut out the lid. Next saw ¼ inch off the front and back of the lid and the box. Cut out the inside space for the box and the lid as indicated by the dotted line, then glue the front and back on the lid and the box.

After the glue dries, hold the lid and box together while you sand and finish it. I usually sand a ¼-inch chamfer on all edges of this type of box by holding the box at about 45 degrees to the belt sander clamped to the workbench.

The hardware is the last thing to put on the box. Add the brass hinges and put a fastener on the lid, if you wish. The little chip-carved design on the lid is optional. You may want to personalize your box by carving an initial or your own design.

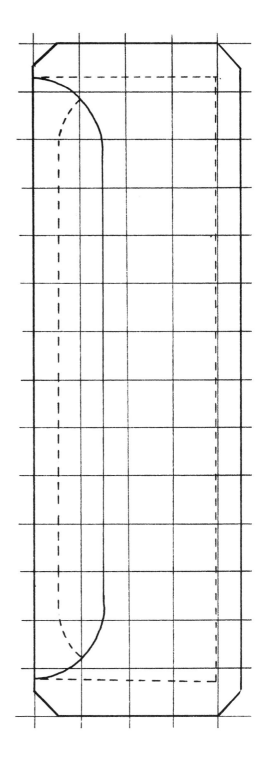

Illus. 32. Cut out the lid first, then saw ¼ inch off the front, back and lid. The dotted line shows the inside space. Carve out the spaces for the two hinges with a sharp knife on the back of the lid, about 1½ inches from each end, and attach them.

Hinged-Lid Box #2

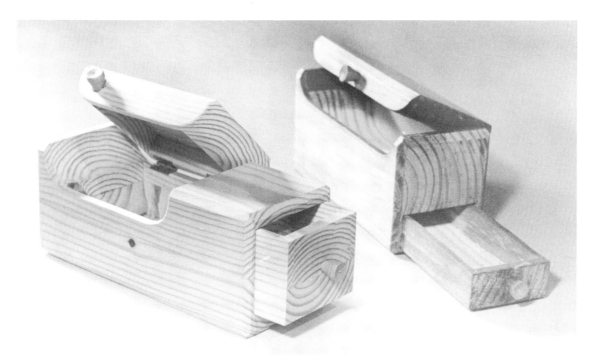

These two hinged-lid boxes are made from two 2 by 4s glued together. For the first box lay the 2 by 4s on their 3½-inch side giving a height of 3 inches and a length of 7½ inches (Illus. 34a). The second stands on the edge of the 2 by 4s to give a height of 3⅓ inches and a length of 6 inches (Illus. 34b).

Although the drawers are of different sizes and positions, the same basic instructions apply to both boxes. Follow the particular illustration for details. First cut out the lid. Then saw ¼ inch off the front and back of the lid and the box using the rip fence on the band saw. Now cut out the inside space of the lid and the box indicated by the dotted lines, and cut out the drawer block. Glue the sides back on the box and lid. Saw ¼ inch off each side of the drawer block and cut out the inside space of the drawer indicated by the dotted lines, and glue the sides back on the drawer.

Carve out the spaces for the hinges on the back of the lid and attach them.

Sand the whole box and apply the finish. Add drawer pulls and lid lift-

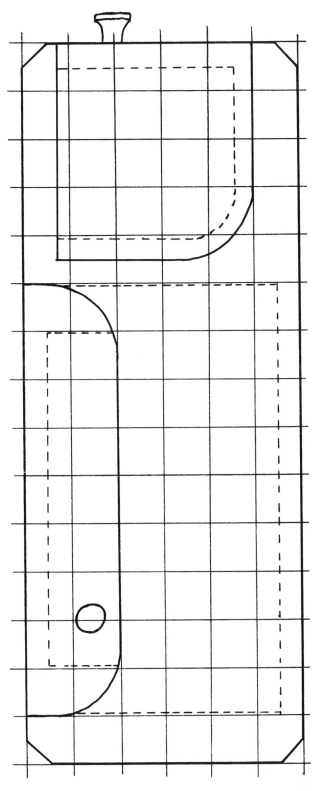

Illus. 34a. First cut out the lid. Then saw ¼ inch off the front and back of the lid. Cut out the inside space of the lid and the drawer space, indicated by the dotted lines. Add the hinges on the back of the lid at each end of the open lid space.

ers. In this case, drill ³⁄₁₆-inch holes in the drawer face and lid, then insert wooden golf tees into the holes. Mark the tees flush on the inside, then remove them and cut at the marks. Put a little glue on the ends of the tees and secure them in the holes.

These boxes can be made in all sizes. You can make them from 2 by 6s glued together.

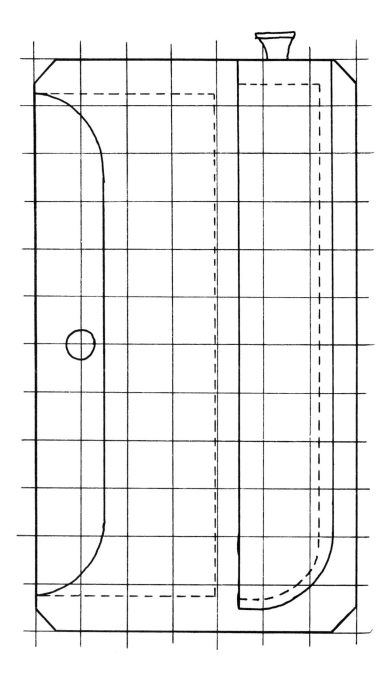

Illus. 34b. Follow the same basic instructions for Illus. 34a. The dotted lines indicate the different drawer spaces.

Hinged-Lid Box #3

This box is technically precise and easy to make. The end result makes it appear as though you really have the corner on precise woodworking.

The dimensions of this box were determined by the need for it to hold 3-by-5 index cards and by the size of the piece of wood I had (Illus. 36a). You can make the box out of any size piece of wood you have—2 by 4s or 2 by 6s glued together make a good-sized box.

First saw ¼ inch off the top of the block, then saw ¼ inch off the front and ⅜ inch off the back using the rip fence. You need the ⅜ inch on the back for the hinges. Now cut out the inside space leaving ¼ inch around the two ends and the bottom. Glue the front and back onto the box, and after it dries glue the top back in place. You now have a hollow block of wood. Sand the block down very nicely, cut the chamfer on the edges if

Illus. 35

you like, and you can even go ahead and put the finish on the box.

Now it gets exciting. Set your band-saw table to an 8-degree bevel, adjust your rip fence about ⅞ inch from the blade. Make sure the bevel slopes to the front of the box, and cut it open (Illus. 36c). Rip a ⅛-inch strip off a piece of scrap and glue the strips inside the box leaving about ³⁄₁₆ inch

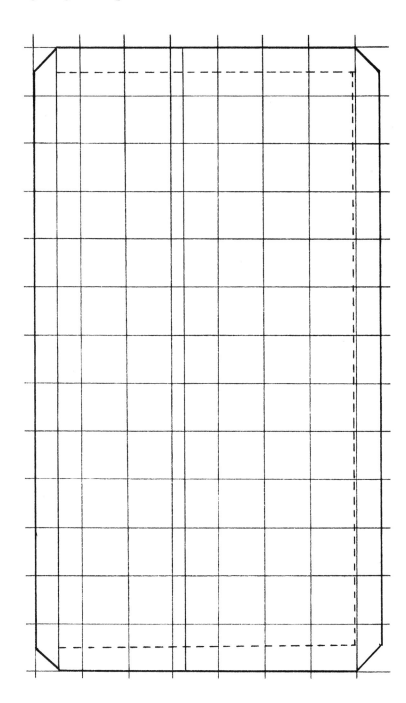

Illus. 36a. First saw ¼ inch off the top of the block (the second solid vertical line from the far left). Then saw ¼ inch off the front and ⅜ inch off the back using a rip fence. Cut along the dotted lines for the inside space.

sticking up. This lets the lid close snugly and also helps the lid stay in position while fitting the hinges.

The optional carving on the lid of the box is, of course, the "evil eye." Anyone trying to invade the secrets held in the box will be subjected to its curse. Lightly carve the design (Illus. 36b) into the lid and accent the edges with a wood-burning tool.

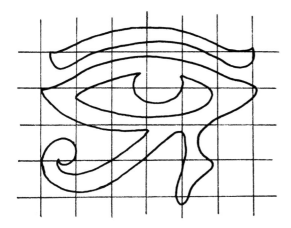

Illus. 36b. The design for the "evil eye."

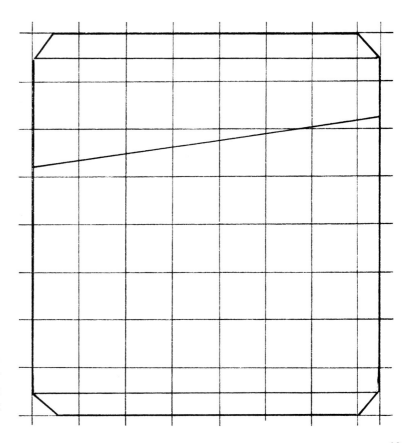

Illus. 36c. Note the diagonal cut for the hinged lid in this side view. Add the hinges about an inch from each end at the high point of the diagonal cut.

Hinged-Lid Box #4

I'm fond of this box because the drawer is in front. This version is 7 inches long, 6 inches deep, and 4½ inches high (Illus. 38). Begin by gluing six pieces of 1-by-8 yellow pine together so the end grain is in front. Turn the pieces around and over to get the end grain arranged in the basket-weave effect. Arrange the grain any way you like. In fact, if you made the box square, you could alternate end grain with edge grain for a nice effect.

Start by sawing ⅜ inch off each side. Then cut out the lid pattern. This is almost the same lid as for a flip-top box, but not quite. With the lid removed, cut out the inside space for the box, then cut out the drawer block and glue the sides back on. Be especially careful to line up the grain pattern in the front of the box.

Next saw ³⁄₁₆–¼ inch off each side of the drawer block, cut out the drawer space indicated by the dotted line, and glue the drawer sides back together. With the lid and drawer in place, sand the front of the box with the belt or pad sander.

Add the little brass hinges (¾ by ⅝ inch) and the drawer pull, in this case a wooden golf tee with the cup part rounded off and glued into a ¼-inch hole drilled through the drawer face. Sand a ¼-inch chamfer on all corners, if you wish.

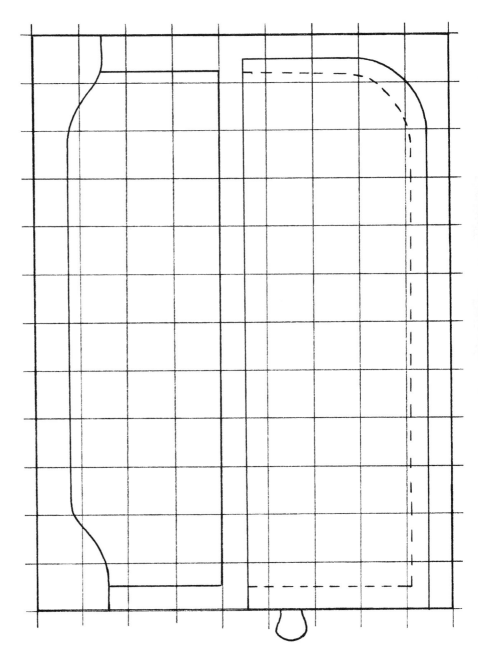

Illus. 38. The side view of this hinged-lid box. Saw ⅜ inch off each side, then cut out the lid pattern (at left). The solid line shows the inside space under the lid; the dotted line shows the inside space for the wide bottom drawer. Add the hinges at the back of the lid (at the top) about an inch from each end.

Breadbox

It was once suggested that this box looks like a loaf of bread. I kind of like that. The box is made of Sitka spruce, which is very expensive and therefore intimidating to use. I didn't buy the spruce; it was given to me by a kindly person.

Begin by sawing the block (in this case, 3½ × 6 × 3 inches) into two pieces at the point where the lid meets the box (Illus. 40a). Then saw ⅜ inch off the front and back of both the box and the lid, which is needed to allow room for rounding the edges and for the hinges. With the sides off, cut out the space inside indicated by the inside solid line. Glue the sides back on the box and the lid.

Some of the rounding of the box can be done on the band saw, especially at the ends. Work down the rest with a hand plane or sand with

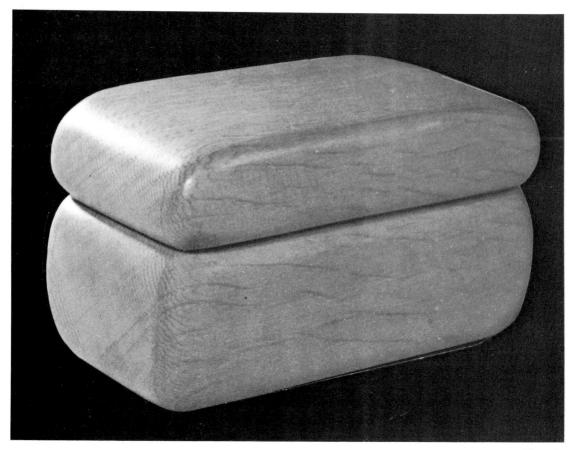

Illus. 39

the belt sander clamped to the workbench. Don't round the back edge where the hinges go, only the back corners. If you round the back edge, you won't have room for the hinges.

The size of this box can be made larger or smaller, but to keep the "loaf-of-bread" look the proportions should remain the same. You are not restricted to making only bread-

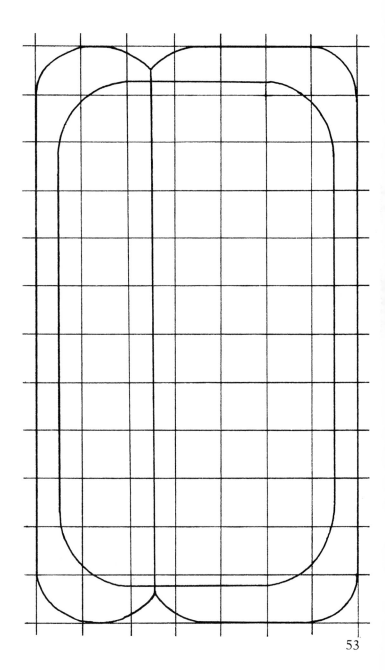

Illus. 40a. The pattern for the front of the breadbox. The lid is at left. See Illus. 40b on the next page for the side pattern.

boxes; the approach can be used on any hinged-lid box you might wish to design.

Finish the box with a light coat of spray varnish and rub linseed oil into the varnish with 0000 steel wool. Never stain expensive wood. Usually the reason the wood is expensive is that it is beautiful in its natural condition.

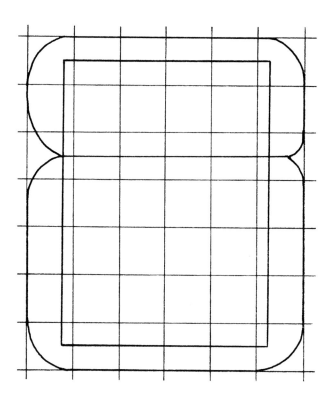

Illus. 40b. The side pattern for the breadbox. The lid is on top. Add the hinges at the back of the lid (at right in the drawing) about an inch from each end.

Footlocker

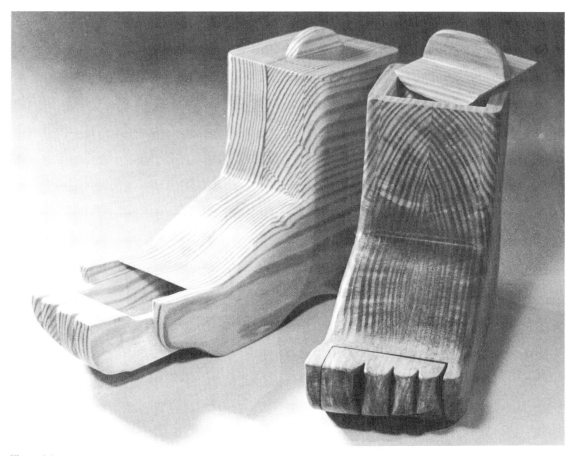

Illus. 41

This is a goofy box, but it's a real conversation piece and fun to make. In making this box, remember that there is a big toe on one side and a little toe on the other, and by the placement of the two outside toes you can make a left foot or a right foot. I made a pair.

Start with two pieces of 2- × 6- × 8-inch yellow pine glued together. Scale up the pattern on one-inch squares and lay it on the block from the big toe side (Illus. 42a). Saw out the shape of the foot first, then saw ⅜ inch off each side of the foot. Next cut out the drawer block and the space in the ankle. Cut out the lid carefully, then saw out the space. Now saw out the shape of the little toe on one of the ⅜-inch sides ripped off the main block of wood (Illus. 42b). Glue the sides back onto the foot. Saw ³⁄₁₆ inch off each side of the drawer block, cut out the drawer space, and reglue the sides.

After the glue has dried, fit the lid and the drawer. Make a cut in the drawer to separate the toes. Shape the bottoms of the toes with the nose of the belt sander and gradually slope from the big toe to the little one.

Illus. 42a. Scale up the pattern on one-inch squares. This is the right side of the footlocker. Note the lid and space to be cut out in the ankle area and the drawer space beginning at the big toe that continues to the heel.

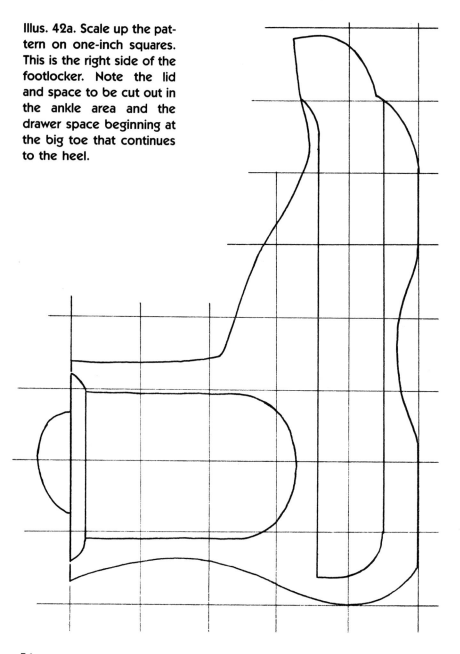

Round all of the edges of the box well since feet have no sharp corners. The darker one in the photograph was stained before varnishing with linseed oil so I could tell the left foot from the right.

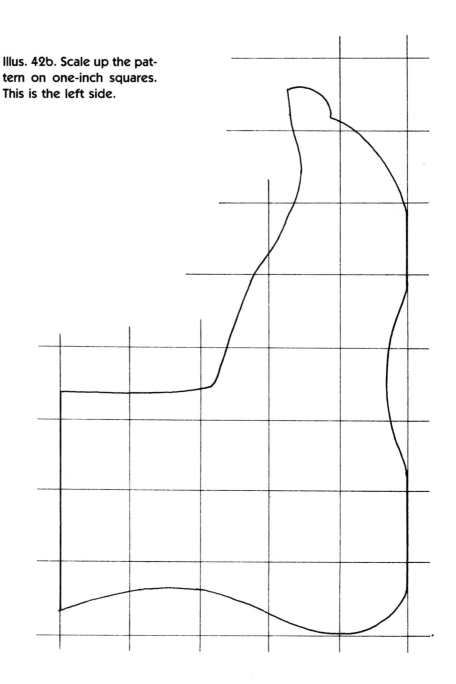

Illus. 42b. Scale up the pattern on one-inch squares. This is the left side.

Lip Box

The lip box is another fun box to make. It scales up or down very nicely and is much easier to make than it might at first appear. It can be made from two 8-inch lengths of 2 by 4 glued together or any larger dimension wood you might have.

Draw the two lips from the pattern (Illus. 44a) on the face of the block of wood, then saw ¼ inch off the back using the rip fence. Starting at the corner of the lips indicated by the dotted lines in the drawing, cut out the top line of the upper lip. Back the saw blade to the entrance kerf and

cut the lower line of the upper lip. Back the blade out of the block and remove the upper lip. Do the same procedure for the lower lip.

To glue up this box, the entrance saw kerf must be closed. There are two ways to do this: one is to put glue in the kerf and clamp it closed, then glue the back on. (This is what I did.) The second method is to cut a ¹⁄₁₆-inch spline and glue it into the kerf before gluing the back on. This method reduces sanding but care must be taken not to let the spline disturb the grain pattern on the face

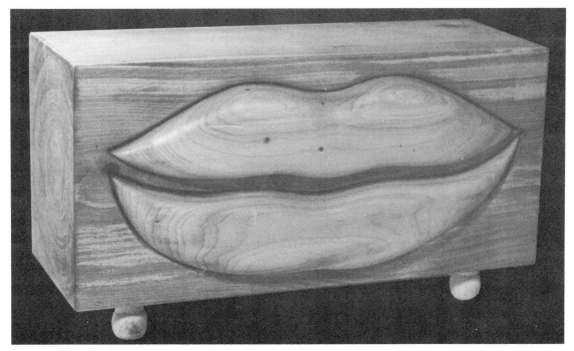

Illus. 43

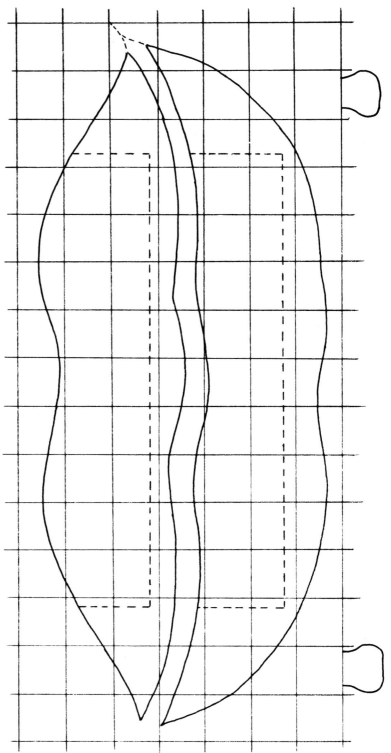

Illus. 44a. The entrance kerf for the shape of the lips is at the top. Cut out the drawer spaces as indicated by the dotted lines. See Illus. 44b on the next page for the side view of the lips.

of the box. After the entrance kerf is closed, glue the back on and clamp up tightly.

Using the rip fence, saw ¼ inch off the back of both lips and ¾ inch off the front of each lip. Cut out drawer space in each lip and glue on the back and front of the lips.

After the glue is dry, cut ½ inch off the front and keep it for a pattern if you intend to make any more lip boxes. Sand the box down well. This is easy since all the sides are flat. When the lips have dried make sure they will slide in and out of the box and that they stick out in front about ½ inch.

Round the corners of the lips to-wards the middle just enough so they are flush with the surface of the box. Then round the edges to approximate the shape of lips (Illus. 44b), with a knife, a chisel, or on the nose of a belt sander clamped to a sawhorse, which is my favorite approach. The lip box usually is more striking in appearance if the lips are stained a different tone from the box.

This box needs feet to raise it enough off the table to allow the lower lip to be pulled out. The best feet I've found are the old-style wooden clothespins. You can still buy them at your local supermarket. Cut about ½ inch off the tops and glue them to the bottom of the box.

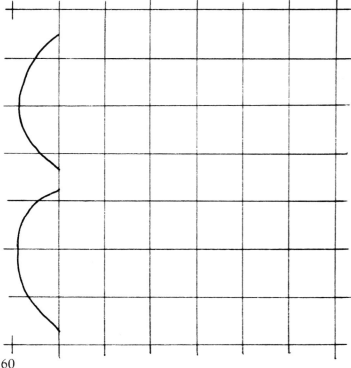

Illus. 44b. Curve the lips in a rounded shape using a knife, chisel, or belt sander.

Whale Box

Illus. 45

The whale box is a simple and quick box to make and the design scales up or down easily. I have made them from 2 by 6s and 2 by 4s, and if your band saw is big enough, you could probably make them out of two 2 by 10s glued together.

Draw the design on the block of wood (Illus. 46a). The lid of the box is hinged on a ⅛-inch dowel that runs all the way through the box. This dowel should be located carefully and the hole drilled square to the surface of the block of wood. A drill press is handy here, but you can mark the hole on each side of the wood and drill halfway through from both sides. Drill the ⅛-inch hole for the hinge dowel and ¼-inch holes about ½ inch deep for the eyes. Insert a short length of ¼-inch dowel in each eyehole and sand it flush.

Now cut out the exterior shape of the whale, including the smile, then saw ¼ inch off each side using the rip fence. Cut out the inside space indi-

Illus. 46a. Drill ¼-inch holes for the eyes (the larger hole at right); drill a ⅛-inch hole (at left) for the hinge dowel. Cut out the inside space as shown by the dotted line.

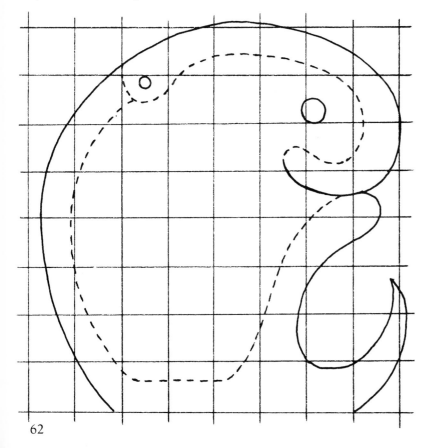

cated by the dotted line. With the space open and the lid free, glue the sides on the body of the whale without the lid. Line the sides up carefully and clamp firmly.

After the glue is dry, fit the lid. Some adjustments to the edges of the lid may be needed to get it to swing freely. If the lid does not open high enough, sand the hinged part of the lid where it meets the body of the whale.

The whale's tail is the only part which needs shaping (Illus. 46b). Cut out the "V" separating the flukes with a knife, and cut the outside shape with a knife or the nose of a belt sander.

The hardest part about the whale is sanding the space between the tail and mouth. A mini-stripper works well, but basically it comes down to sticking your finger in there with a small piece of sandpaper until it's smooth. Stain the box, if you wish, and finish to your liking.

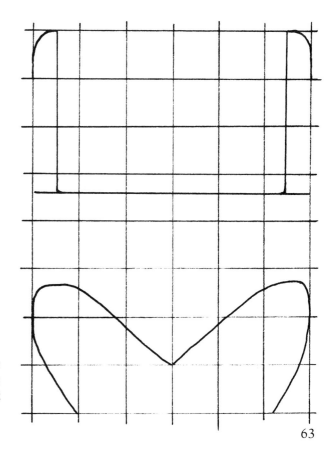

Illus. 46b. The back view of the whale box. Shape the tail with a knife or the nose of a belt sander.

Pig Box

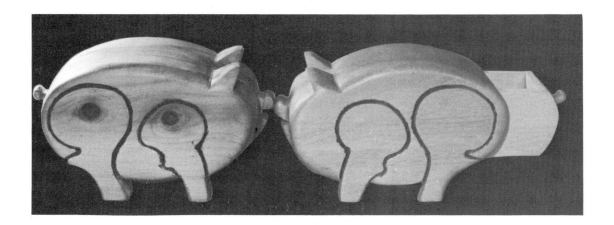

The pig is made from a block of wood 7 inches long, 3½ inches high, and 3 inches wide. This amounts to two 7-inch pieces of 2 by 4 glued together. Draw the profile of the pig on the 3½-inch side of the block (Illus. 48a). Be sure to include the drawer-locator marks on the top, bottom, and sides of the block so they will remain after the sides have been cut off. Or you can simply draw the locator marks around the block's sides and ends with a square.

Using the rip fence, saw ⅜ inch off each side of the block. With a square relocate the position and size of the drawer, then cut out the drawer block.

Now you can glue the sides back on the block of wood using the grain pattern and the drawer-locator marks to reposition the sides. Clamp tightly every few inches to achieve as fine a glue line as possible. When the box is shaped, sanded, and finished the glue should be almost invisible.

Saw ¼ inch off each side of the drawer block using the rip fence. With the drawer block on its side, cut out the space for the inside of the drawer as indicated by the dotted line in the drawing. Glue the sides of the drawer back on.

After the glue has dried on the block, put the drawer in position and cut out the profile of the pig. Much of the shaping of the nose, mouth, and tail is done on a band saw (Illus. 48b).

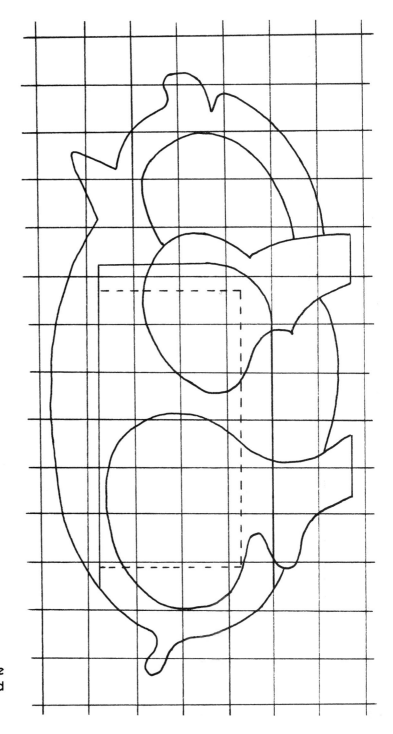

Illus. 48a. Cut out the drawer space as indicated by the dotted line.

The space between the ears is cut with a knife or chisel and the space separating the legs is shaped with a drum sander or the nose of a belt sander.

The shape of the legs and joints can be relieved with a router, but no deeper than ¼ inch. The pigs shown here had their legs drawn on with a wood-burning tool.

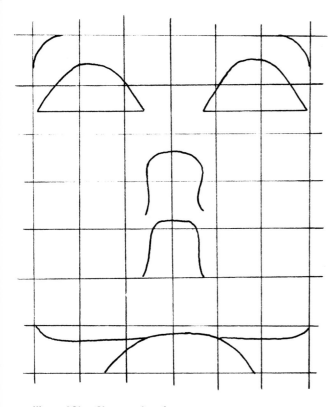

Illus. 48b. Shape the face of the pig with a knife or chisel.

Turtle Box

The turtle box is a favorite design of many people. The size is about the same as the average turtle you find on the side of the road and the pose is that of a turtle going as fast as it can.

Glue together two 8-inch lengths of 2 by 4 with the glue line horizontal, which is 3 inches high and 3½ inches wide. Draw the profile on the block of wood and cut it out (Illus. 50a). Saw ⅜ inch off each side using the rip fence. Take the two sides and saw off the head, neck, and tail, but not the legs. Now cut out the drawer block starting at the base of the neck along the top of the block (Illus. 50b). Back the blade out and start cutting at the bottom line of the drawer, around the curve, and up to the first cut until the block is free.

Glue the sides onto the turtle's body lining up the grain carefully and clamp tightly.

Saw ³⁄₁₆–¼ inch off each side of the drawer block, cut out the drawer space, and glue the sides back on the drawer.

After the glue dries, the shape of the head and neck can be cut on the drawer (Illus. 50c). Whittle the tail down to proper size. Cut the line indicating the separation between the legs and the shell with a knife or use a small disc sander on your electric drill. Cut out the space separating the legs with the nose of a belt or drum sander. Round all edges of the body and sand the whole turtle sufficiently. Finish with varnish and rub with linseed oil and 0000 steel wool.

Illus. 49

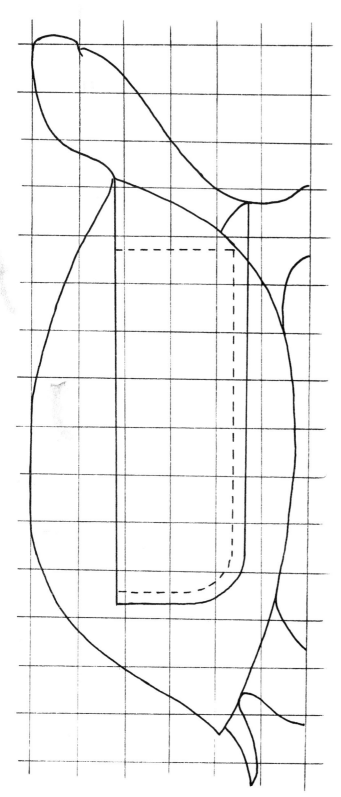

Illus. 50a. Cut out the drawer space as indicated by the dotted line.

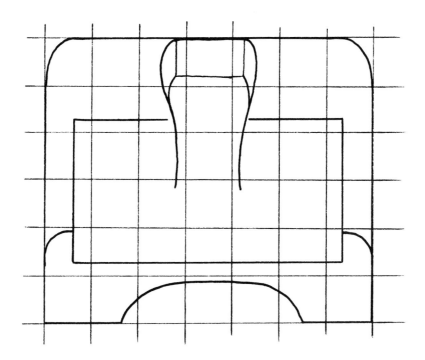

Illus. 50b. The front view of the turtle. Cut out the drawer block starting along the line above the neck.

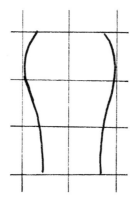

Illus. 50c. Shape the head as shown in this bird's-eye view.

Duck Box

Here we have a sleeping duck. This box is simpler to make than it looks, even though it does require a little of the old "cut-and-look" technique.

Scale the pattern up to ¾-inch squares. This will produce a duck box close to the actual size of a real duck, about 9½ inches long and 3¼ inches wide. Start with a block about 10 inches long, 3½ inches high, and 3½ inches wide.

Draw the duck in profile on the block of wood and saw to shape all outside lines (Illus. 52a). Saw ⅜ inch off both sides with the rip fence. To get the drawer block out, start the saw cut at the end of the bill and cut between the head and the body to the line at the top of the drawer block, then back the blade out. Start the second cut at the bottom line of the

drawer block at the base of the neck, cutting around to meet the first saw cut, and the drawer block is free, including the neck, head, and bill.

Glue the sides of the duck back onto the body. Saw ¼ inch off each side of the drawer block and cut out the drawer space. Then glue the sides back on the drawer.

After the glue is dry, cut out the shape of the duck's body and neck as viewed from the top (Illus. 52b) by holding the drawer in position.

Sand all edges of the body until

Illus. 52a. (right) Scale up the pattern on ¾-inch squares. Cut out the drawer space as indicated by the dotted line. **Illus. 52b. (far right)** Cut out the shape of the duck's body as viewed from the top.

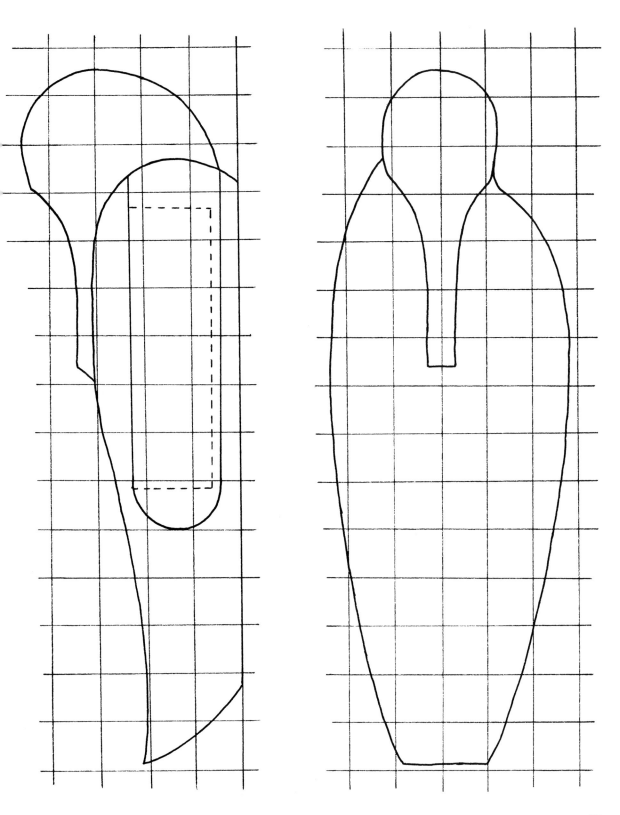

they are rounded and smooth. Whittle the head and neck with a knife or chisel. Use a light touch with a drum sander or belt sander to smooth out the lumps, then it's down to hand sanding. One of the best ways to sand end grain, as you'll find on the back of the duck's neck, is to hold the drawer between your knees and use a 4-inch strip of sandpaper as though you were shining your shoes. Stain, rub with linseed oil, and wax to finish.

Fir Croc Box

This box is a flip-top type. By closing the croc's mouth, the back is raised, revealing the space indicated by the dotted line (Illus. 54a). This all pivots on a ¼-inch dowel, which is the eye. The croc is made of fir which, after the croc is finished, is burned with a propane torch, then wire-brushed to remove the ashes and relieve the grain. No other finish is applied.

Glue two 12½-inch-long 2 by 4s together. Enlarge the pattern to ¾-inch squares, then draw it on the 3-inch dimension. Drill the eye out first. Then cut out the profile shape including the teeth. Now saw ⅜ inch off each side. Cut off the two sides of the mouth leaving the shape of the head. Cut out the lid including the upper jaw and the inside space of the main body. Glue the sides back on the body.

Cut out the shape of the upper jaw on the lid as shown in Illus. 54c. After the glue dries, cut out the shape of the lower jaw and tail as indicated in Illus. 54b. While the lid and body are still in two pieces, cut out the space between the teeth in the mouth with a gouge or a sander. Fit and assemble the lid to the body with a length of ¼-inch dowel, but before cutting the dowel flush make sure everything works.

Illus. 53

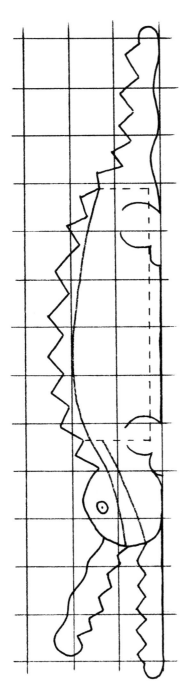 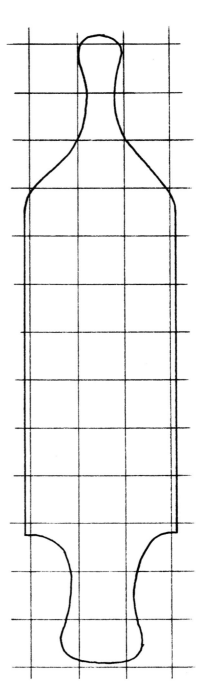

Illus. 54a. Scale up the pattern on ¾-inch squares. Drill a ¼-inch hole through the eye; the lid hinges here with a ¼-inch dowel. Cut out the drawer space as indicated by the dotted line.

Illus. 54b. The lower jaw and tail section of the fir croc. (Scale up to ¾-inch squares.)

Now sand it all down, carve the little legs and finish to your liking. The burning procedure works well on fir and yellow pine. The yellow pine will stay quite dark. This burning business makes the croc look more reptilian, and it saves you from having to sand all those humps in his back.

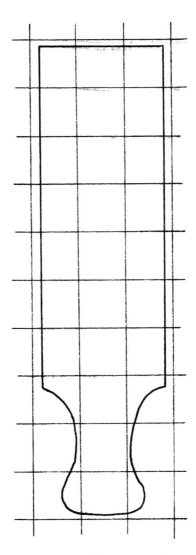

Illus. 54c. The upper jaw and lid section. (Scale up to ¾-inch squares.)

Fir Hare Box

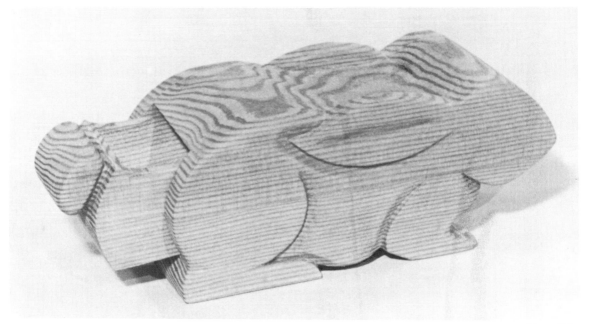

This rabbit box may look complicated, but it's actually fairly easy to make if you follow the instructions step by step. The box is made of fir, because it's natural for a rabbit—pun intended. Any other wood you might have would also work quite well.

Start with two pieces of fir glued together that are each $2 \times 4 \times 7\frac{1}{2}$ inches long. Draw the shape of the rabbit on the 3-inch side of the wood and cut it out. Using your rip fence, slice $\frac{3}{8}$ inch off each side of the rabbit. The curved dotted line in the drawing (Illus. 56) between the head and the hind quarters indicates the space between the rabbit's ears. Cut out that wedge after the sides have been sawn off. Now cut out the

drawer block. Next saw off the tail sections from each of the two cutoff sides along the dotted line. Glue the sides back on the rabbit.

Saw $\frac{3}{16}$ inch off the sides of the drawer block and then cut the tail sections off them. Cut out the drawer space indicated by the dotted line and glue the sides back in place. You should now have a rabbit with space between its ears and a tail that is not quite as wide as the drawer.

To carve out the details for the legs, ears, and under the chin, it is easiest to use a knife, making vertical incisions along the lines at least $\frac{1}{16}$ inch deep. Then slant the knife towards the incisions and cut out little ribbons of wood. With the rabbit clamped to the

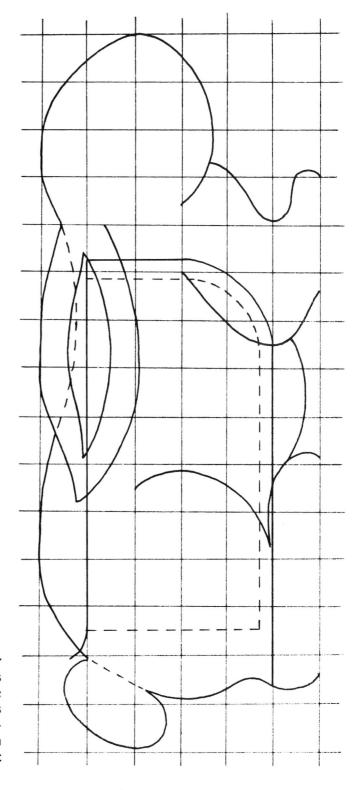

Illus. 56. Cut out the drawer space in the rabbit's body as shown by the dotted line. The dotted line by the ear shows where the wood is cut away between them; give the tail a rounded shape—but don't cut it completely off.

bench, use a small disc sander in your electric drill to carefully sand the cut-out grooves. Make sure the grooves are less than ⅜ inch; otherwise you will sand into the drawer.

Cut out the hollow that runs the length of the ear down the middle from point to point. Then sand out the rest of the hollow.

Sand down the edges of the rabbit by hand, then apply a finish of your choice. My fir hare was simply soaked in linseed oil and then set out to air for a few days.

Jumper Box

This box has been dubbed the "jumper" because it looks as if it might do just that. It is made of two 2 by 4s, 4½ inches long, glued together.

Draw the pattern on the block and

Illus. 57

cut out the profile of the box, then saw ¼ inch off each side using the rip fence (Illus. 58a). Cut out the drawer block and glue the sides back on the box using lots of clamps. Saw ³⁄₁₆–¼ inch off each side of the drawer block, cut out the drawer space, then glue the sides back on the drawer. Fit the drawer into the box and sand the whole thing. The drawer pull is a wooden golf tee. Drill a ³⁄₁₆-inch hole at the location of the drawer pull and push a tee in as far as it will go before you mark the tee inside the drawer. Cut the tee off at the mark, add a little glue, and push it back into the hole.

Cut the line on the side of the box indicating the jumper's "thigh" in relief with a knife or a small disc sander in an electric drill. To cut out the space between the legs, place the jumper face down on the saw table and saw up the inside of both legs to the curvature of the body, then between the legs (Illus. 58b). This will make the cut just right on the front as well.

Because of the grain direction in the feet, they are easy to break. If a foot breaks, just glue it together. The glue will make the foot stronger and it will probably not break again.

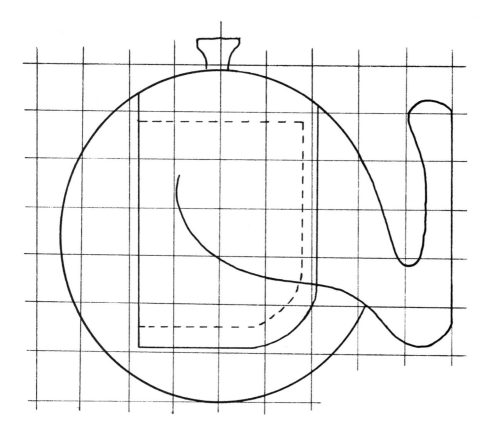

Illus. 58a. Cut out the drawer space as shown by the dotted line in this side view.

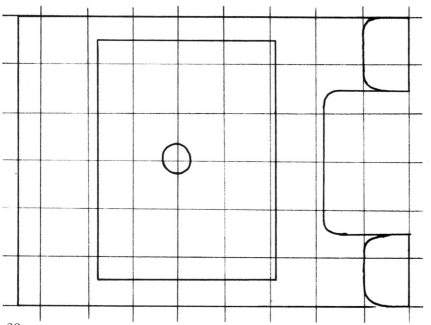

Illus. 58b. The front view of the jumper box. The circle represents the drawer pull (golf tee).

Walker Box

This box comes under the category of "fanciful creature." It turns out well in the size in the drawing, or larger, as the one in the photograph. The box is cut from two pieces of 2 by 4 or 2 by 6 glued together. The legs are cut from a separate piece of 1 by 4 or 1 by 6. You will need two sets of legs, of course, one set for each side.

Draw the circle for the body on the block of wood with a compass so you can find the exact center. Drill a ¼-inch hole about ½ inch into the block of wood at the center on each side, to locate the legs. Next drill the hole for the dowel to hinge the lid. If the box is drawn from the given scale (Illus. 60a), a ⅛-inch dowel will be fine. If the box is 5 inches in diameter or bigger, a ¼-inch dowel is more suitable. This hole must go all the way through the block.

Cut out the circle and saw ¼ inch off each side of the block. Starting at the hinged end of the lid, cut around the hole as far as possible, then back the blade out and cut from the opening end of the lid to meet the first cut. With the lid removed, cut out the inside space of the box and glue the sides back in place. After the glue is dry, fit the lid. The knob for lifting the lid is a wooden golf tee, which you mark, cut, and glue into a ³⁄₁₆-inch hole.

Trace the pattern for the legs on 1-by-4 or 1-by-6 material and mark the center (Illus. 60b). Drill a ¼-inch hole at the center and cut out the legs. Sand the box and the legs before they are assembled. If you wish to stain

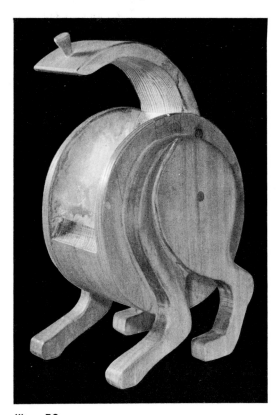

Illus. 59

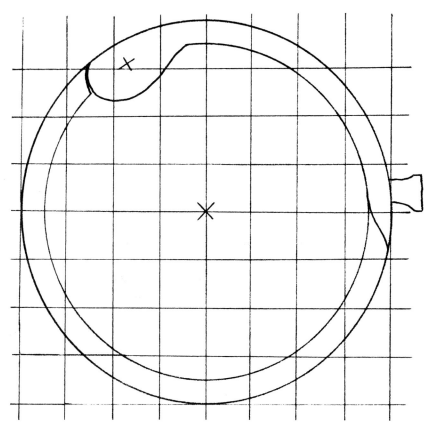

Illus. 60a. Drill a ⅛-inch hole through the box at the top for the hinged lid; drill ¼-inch holes about ½ inch deep into the middle to locate the legs, as shown by the crosses.

Illus. 60b. Drill ¼-inch holes through both sets of legs, indicated by the cross, and attach to the box with two pieces of inch-long ¼-inch dowel.

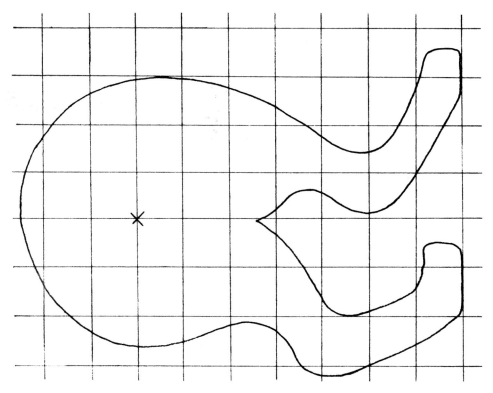

the box and legs in different shades, do this also before assembly.

Fit the legs to the box with pieces of ¼-inch dowel about an inch long before gluing just to see how they fit. The legs can be rotated independently on the dowel. Set the box on a flat surface and adjust the legs so all four feet touch it. Now remove the legs, add glue, and readjust and clamp the legs in place until the glue is dry.

High-Rise Box

This box is surprisingly quick and easy to make. It can be made from a tree root, 2 by 4s, or plywood. The box in Illus. 61 was made from a 10-inch piece of elm root.

Square the block first by using a hatchet and a hand plane to get one flat side. Then lay a square on the flat side to square the ends, drawing chalk lines to get straight lines from end to end on each side. Place the flat side on the band-saw table and saw along the chalk lines and you have three flat, mostly parallel sides. Draw a line along the fourth side and cut it.

The block, after sanding and a little squaring, should be 3¾ inches square and 10 inches tall. Enlarge the pattern to ½-inch squares and draw it on the block (Illus. 62). Saw ¼ inch off the back using the rip fence. Cut out the three drawer blocks by sawing in from the side and out the same side. Glue the back into place, and saw ⅜ inch off the front and ¼ inch off the back of each drawer block. Cut out the inside space of the drawers and glue the front and back onto each drawer. Be sure to get the correct front and back on the drawer.

After the glue has dried, cut out the outside shape from the front. Now the sanding begins. Wherever the sides of the box curve in, the front also curves in, but not as much.

Shape the curves on the nose of a belt sander and with drum sanders on an electric drill. Round the drawer faces and all edges of the box around the drawers. For drawer pulls use simple little shapes cut from a scrap of the same wood. They can be any shape you like.

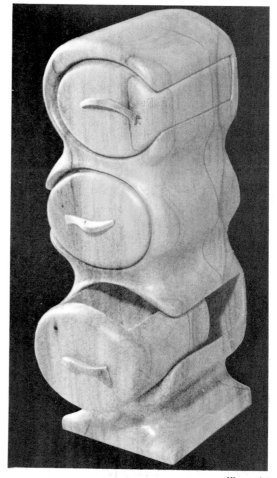

Illus. 61

84

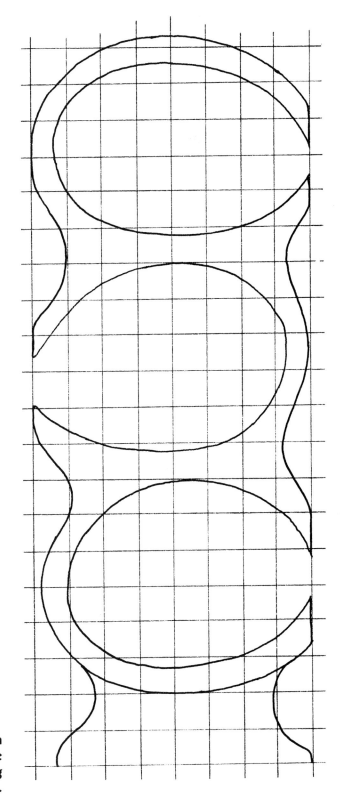

Illus. 62. Scale up the pattern on ½-inch squares. Cut out the three drawer blocks by entering and exiting from the open sides.

Underwater Box

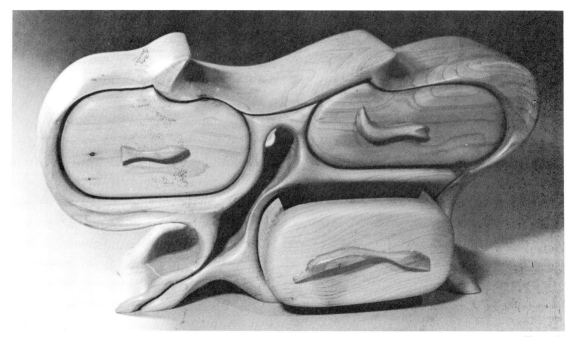

This box was made from a piece of cedar rescued from a dying tree in front of my house. It's a nice box, which can be made from just about any kind of wood.

Draw the pattern on ¾-inch squares and transfer it to the face of the block (Illus. 64). The box is 10 inches long, 5 inches high, and 3¾ inches deep. First saw ⅜ inch off the back. The drawer blocks are cut out next, and this is a little tricky. Start the saw cut in the lower right corner of the bottom drawer. Cut out the block around completely and remove it. For the upper-right drawer block, cut around the right end of the drawer up to the peak. Turn the saw off and back the wood into the first drawer space with the blade turned around and backed into the kerf. Saw along the bottom of the drawer around the left end until you meet the cut at the peak from the opposite direction. Now remove the second drawer block, and, using the same procedure, saw out the left drawer block.

Glue the back on the block of wood and cut out the outside shape of the box. To cut out the oxygen bubble rising to the surface, drill a ½-inch hole at the top and saw to it.

To make the drawers, saw ½ inch off the front and ³⁄₁₆ inch off the back

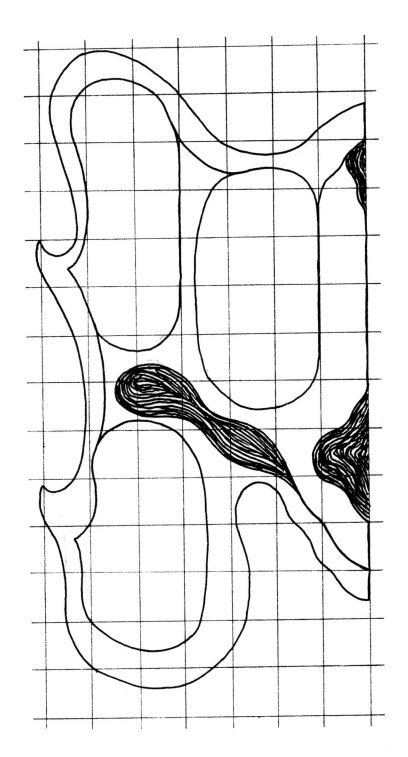

Illus. 64. Scale up the pattern on ¾-inch squares. Cut out the darkened areas completely.

of each block, then cut out the drawer space and glue the drawers back together. Glue a small piece of veneer into the kerf well below the surface so it is not visible.

There is a great deal of sanding and shaping involved with this box. The idea is to make the box appear to have a flowing motion, which means no sharp corners or regular shapes.

Varnish and rub the box with linseed oil and 0000 steel wool.

Madonna-and-Child Box

The upper drawer of this box seems to be protecting the lower drawer—hence "the madonna and child." It may sound a bit grandiose, but it sounds better than "mom and the kid."

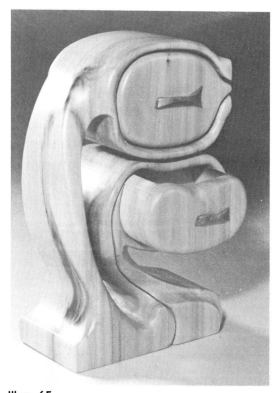

Illus. 65

Start with a 5- × 8- × 3-inch block of poplar. Transfer the pattern (Illus. 66) on the face and cut ⅜ inch off the back. Cut out the top drawer block by entering from the side as you did for the high-rise box. Cut out the lower drawer block by sawing up from the bottom and around the drawer. After the drawer blocks are removed, glue the back on the block and cut out the shape of the box. Saw ¼ inch off the fronts and backs of the drawer blocks and cut out the drawer space. Then glue the drawers back together.

Glue a spline into the saw kerf at the base of the box to make sure it doesn't close. Shape the rest of the box with a knife, belt and drum sanders, and, of course, lots of hand sanding in the end. If you like to sand, this is a good box for you to make. Glue shims to the bottoms of the drawers to help even out the space between the drawers and the box.

The drawer pulls are pieces of fungus-stained elm. To finish, use varnish and rub with linseed oil and 0000 steel wool.

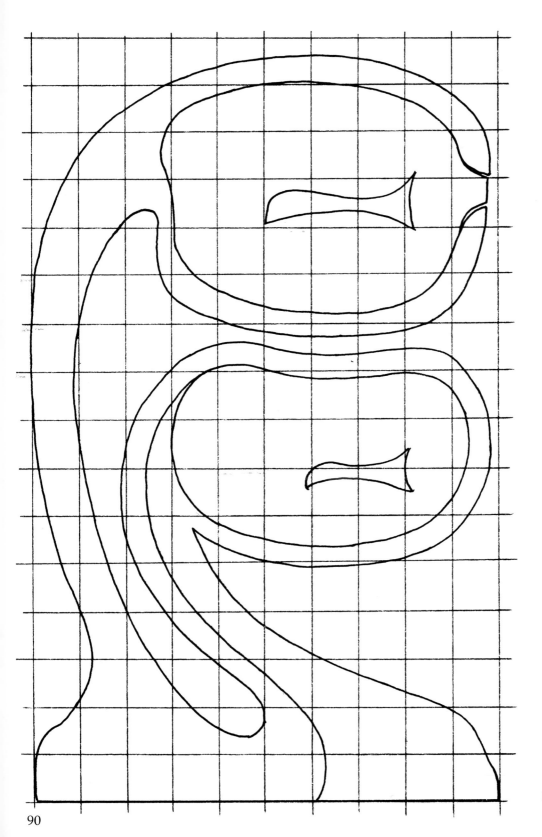

Illus. 66

Pod Box

This is a poplar box, so named because the two upper drawers look like pods growing at the ends of stalks.

The box is 10½ inches high, 5

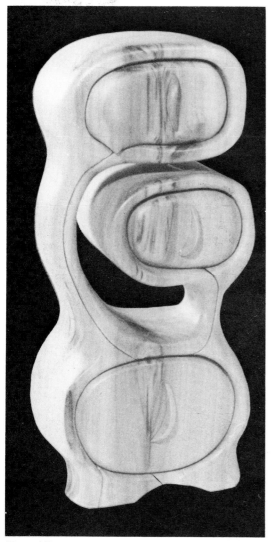

inches wide, and 3 inches deep. Begin by drawing the pattern (Illus. 69 enlarged to ¾-inch squares) on the front and sawing ⅜ inch off the back using the rip fence. Cut out the drawer blocks by starting at the bottom left side, then cut out the other two drawer blocks as indicated. Glue the back on and cut out the shape of the box. Make the drawers in the usual manner and shape the rest of it with a belt sander and drum sanders. Round the drawer faces of the two upper drawers well. Leave the bottom drawer face basically flat because it's fairly large.

Glue the saw kerf shut at the bottom. Bevel the kerf a little with a knife to accent the line. Varnish and oil the box to finish it.

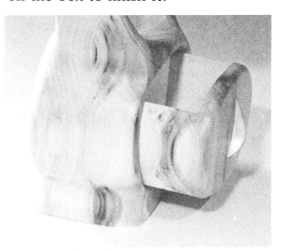

Illus. 67

Illus. 68. A side view of the pod box.

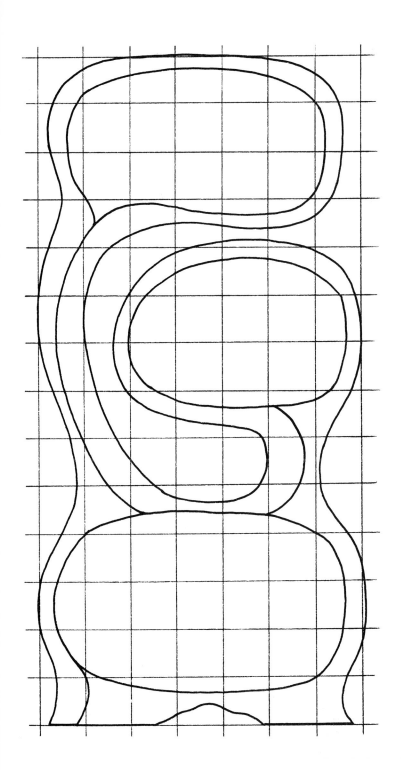

Illus. 69. Scale up the pattern on ¾-inch squares. Cut out the lower drawer block first, then travel up the wavy line to cut out the top blocks.

Fantasy Box

Once upon a time, a tower of light rose high above a faraway land of darkness. In this tower lived the Seer, a person who saw mysteries, knew secret things, and made band-saw boxes. He made this box from a piece of 10¾- × 5- × 2¾-inch poplar.

Scale up the pattern on ¾-inch squares and transfer it to the front of the block of wood (Illus. 71). Then saw ¼ inch off the back. Cut out the lower drawer block by sawing down the right side of the far left mountain peak. After the lower drawer block is removed, saw along the wavy line up the tower and remove the high drawer block. Then glue the back on the block and cut out the shape from the front. Carve the pointed, hard edges into the poplar with a knife and sand the tower smooth. Open the saw kerf, which winds its way up the tower, with a knife to show the path leading to the high drawer.

When you are ready to finish the box, start at the base and put a dark stain between the mountain peaks and deep in the valleys and around the edges of the lower drawer. Use a lighter stain all around the rest of the base. As you move up the tower, make the stain lighter and lighter until the upper part and the top drawer are the natural light color of the poplar. Then spray the whole box with varnish and rub it with linseed oil and 0000 steel wool.

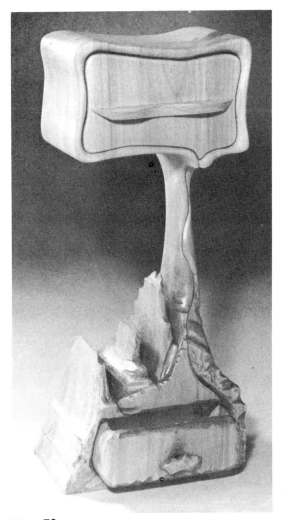

Illus. 70

93

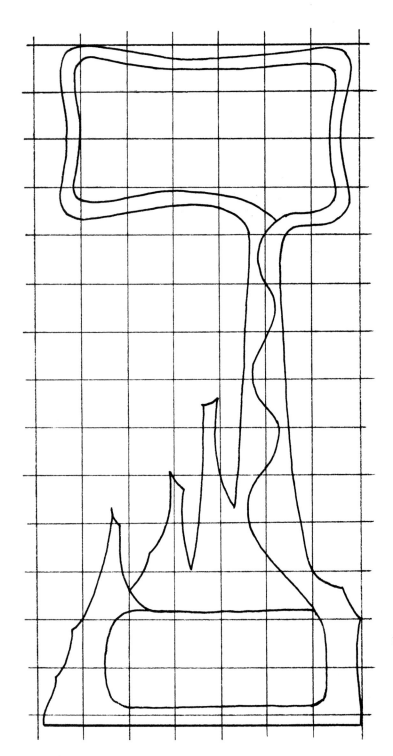

Illus. 71. Scale up the pattern on ¾-inch squares. Cut out the lower block first by entering along the far-left mountain peak. Then travel up the wavy line to cut out the top block.

Twined Box

This box is 8¾ inches high, 5 inches wide, and 3 inches deep. It is made of poplar, with the box stained dark and the drawers stained a lighter tone.

Draw the design on ¾-inch squares (Illus. 73), then transfer the pattern to the block of wood (two 2 by 6s glued together will work as well as a single block of wood). Use a ⅛-inch 15-tooth blade to saw out the box and drawers. Saw ¼ inch off the back of the wood and cut out the drawer blocks starting from the side and around the drawer block to the point at the bottom. Back the blade out of the kerf and turn the wood so you can saw in the other direction. Saw around the top and right end and down to the drawer point. When both drawer blocks are free glue the back on the block. Glue a spline in the kerf.

While the glue is drying you can make the drawers. Saw ³⁄₁₆–¼ inch off the back and ⅜ inch off the front. Mark the drawer space and saw out, then glue the front and back onto the drawers.

Now shape the outside of the box. First cut out the space that is totally enclosed by drilling a ⅜-inch hole at each of the four corners, then use a sabre saw or a keyhole saw to remove the rest of the wood.

Getting the twined part to look right is a matter of cutting and looking. Begin with a flat chisel and dig as deeply as you like. Smooth the edges with a knife and use a disc sander on your electric drill to clean out the chisel marks.

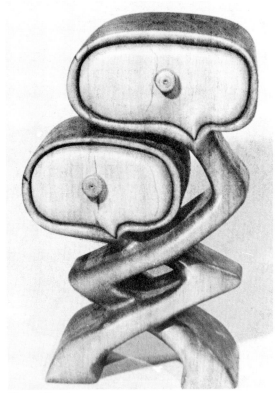

Illus. 72

95

When all the basic shaping is done there is nothing left to do but sand, mostly by hand. With several sheets of 80-grit, 100-grit, 150-grit, and even some 220-grit paper, sand the entire box in graduated steps. This does not need to be done in one sitting. It usually works best if it isn't. When all is sanded, stain, varnish, and rub with 0000 steel wool and linseed oil.

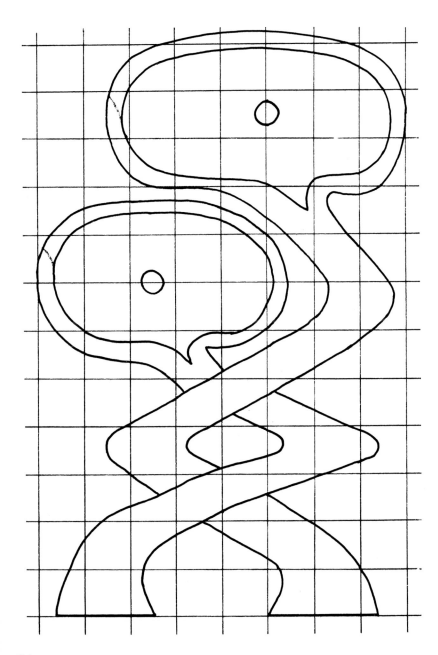

Illus. 73. Scale up the pattern on ¾-inch squares. Cut out the drawer blocks by entering at the indicated kerf lines at left.

Kitty-Cornered Box

This box is strange to look at and very hard to figure out how to make. Looking at the drawing doesn't help a lot, either, but it will all be clear after you read this. I hope.

The box is two 7½-inch-long pieces of 2 by 4 glued together. Since the

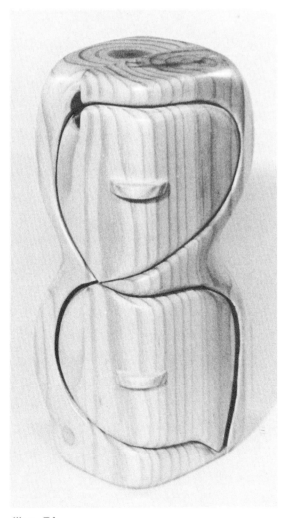

front and back of the box are corners, you need to saw ¼ inch off two adjoining sides. The heavy middle line in the drawing (Illus. 75) is the front corner of the box. Align the middle line up with the corner, fold the paper around the box, tape it in place, then transfer the drawing onto the wood with carbon paper. The reason the drawing looks odd is that the shape is laid out flat when, in fact, it represents a curved shape. After the drawing is wrapped around the box, it looks like it's supposed to.

Cut out the drawer blocks with great care because the back corner is the only part of the box that touches the saw tables. This means that the block can tilt to either side. Hold it vertical as well as you can. It's not that critical. One very critical point, however, is that there is "open" blade below the box, which means you must not keep your fingers under the box. *Keep all your fingers in sight at all times.* If you can see them, you won't saw them.

Cut the drawer blocks out in the figure-8 shape. Glue a ¹⁄₁₆-inch spine in the entrance kerf and glue the two sides back in place.

Make the drawers by sawing the front and back off the drawer blocks. This involves holding the block vertically straight and sawing ¼ inch

Illus. 74

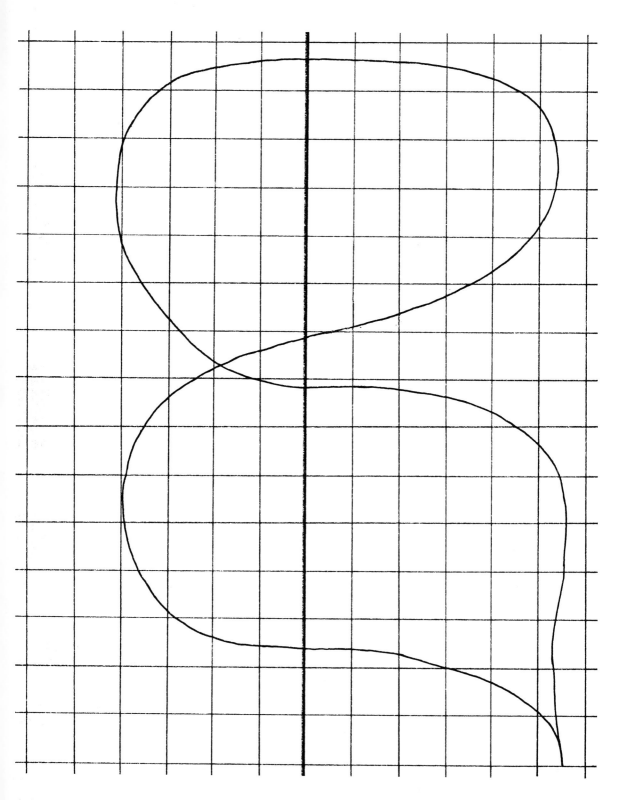

around the front corner and the same around the back corner. Then cut out the drawer space and glue the front and back on the drawers.

Shape the outside of the box on the belt sander clamped to the bench. Since you are sanding corners, the sander cuts very quickly so check occasionally to be sure you are not about to sand into the drawers.

This box was made of yellow pine 2 by 4s and no stain was used. Sand it well, apply varnish, then rub with steel wool and linseed oil.

Illus. 75. The heavy line in the middle is the front corner of the box. Fold the pattern around the box with carbon paper to transfer the design.

Marble Boxes

Wood taken from tree crotches usually has attractive, swirling designs. From a dead elm tree I saved such a piece, and after much sawing, hacking, and sanding I had a beautiful 8- × 5- × 4¾-inch block of fungus-stained elm. The black lines are fungus stains, which make the wood look like marble—hence these "marble boxes."

Since this wood is not easy to come by, you shouldn't waste any of it. Here's a plan to make three marble boxes from one block of wood.

The first box is exactly the size of the original block. (Enlarge the patterns in Illus. 78, 79, and 80 to ¾-inch squares). Marble box #1 (Illus. 76) is a hinged-lid box. Saw ½ inch off the top, front, and back in that order. Be-

Illus. 77

fore cutting out the inside space, drill two holes ⅜ inch in diameter in the bottom corners so you can saw to the holes, turn the blade 90 degrees in the hole, and saw on. This saves a lot of wood and it puts a nice detail on the remaining block.

Glue the sides and top back on the original block, round the front edge of the lid, and cut a lifting tab into it. Sand the box well, then cut it open with the band-saw table set at the angle shown in the drawing (Illus. 78b). Add hinges and glue a lip to the inside of the box. Then varnish and rub with linseed oil.

The block which you are left with after making the first box is 7 × 4 × 3⅜ inches. Box #2 is similar to a hinged-lid box except there are no hinges (Illus. 77). Cut open the lid

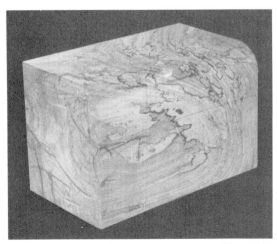

Illus. 76

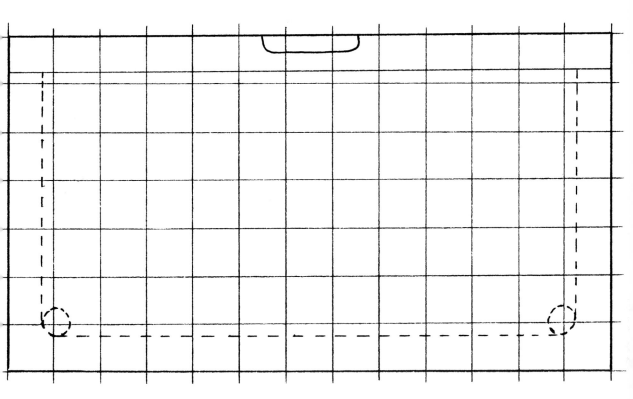

Illus. 78a. (above) Scale up both patterns on ¾-inch squares. Before cutting out the inside space, drill two ⅜-inch holes so you can turn the blade 90 degrees to make the cut.

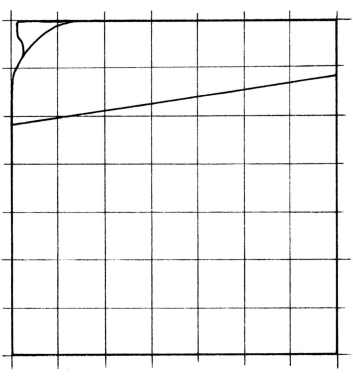

Illus. 78b. Cut out the lid of the box at the angle as shown in this side view. Add the hinges about an inch from each end at the top of the diagonal cut.

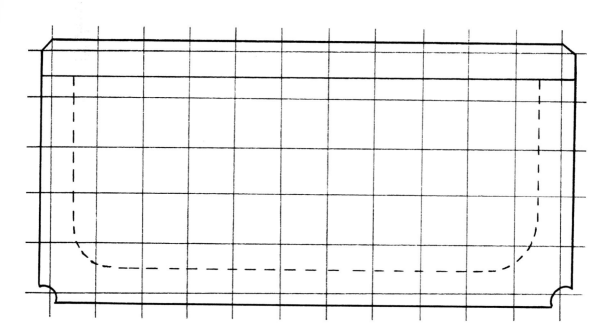

Illus. 79. Scale up both patterns on ¾-inch squares. Cut out the lid and the inside space as indicated by the dotted lines. Glue a lip that will hold the lid in place on the inside of all four sides.

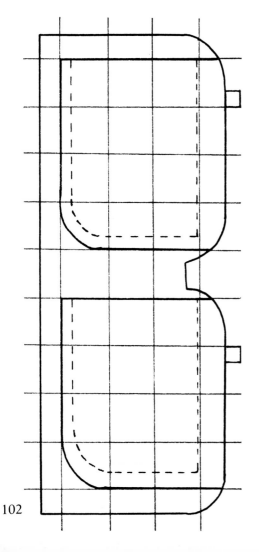

Illus. 80. The side view of the marble box shown in Illus. 81. Cut out the drawer spaces as indicated by the dotted lines.

102

squarely instead of at an angle and glue the lip to the inside on all four sides. Sand a ¼-inch chamfer around the lid of the box.

Cut out the inside space with 1¼-inch-diameter corners, which form the top and bottom profile of the third box. Use a 1¼-inch diameter because that is the minimum diameter a ¼-inch blade will cut.

The third box is a standard two-drawer box, but first cut the profile shape, then saw ¼ inch off both sides. Cut out the drawer blocks and glue the sides back (Illus. 80). Cut ³⁄₁₆ inch off both sides of the drawer blocks, cut out the drawer spaces, and glue the drawer sides back. Make drawer pulls from the wood cut out of the drawer space.

The only pieces of wood left from the whole operation are the two little pieces which came out of the drawer spaces. Don't throw them away. They make interesting, contrasting drawer pulls for other boxes.

Varnish the first and third boxes and rub with linseed oil; wax the second box with Johnson's floor wax.

Illus. 81

Stump Box

This is perhaps not the best name for this box. It was made from the stump of a red cedar tree, but since it no longer looks like a stump maybe it should be called a cedar canister. It doesn't have to be cedar, either. The wood can be about anything you have, but it must be well seasoned or the lid of the box will warp.

The dimensions of this box are 6 inches high and 6 inches in diameter. These dimensions are not critical to the design or the procedure. You can make the box as small as you wish or as big as your band saw will cut (the pattern in Illus. 83a is for a 3½-inch box).

The technique for making the canister is quite simple. Take a piece of tree trunk or limb the length of the box you want to make and saw off both ends square. With a compass draw a circle the diameter of the canister and cut it out. This will remove

Illus. 82

104

all the bark and give you parallel sides. Drill a hole in the top for a dowel on which the lid will hinge. The hole should go through the lid and about an inch into the body of the canister. If it is a large canister, say 5 or 6 inches in diameter, use a ¼-inch dowel and a ¼-inch hole. For smaller canisters use a ³⁄₁₆- or ⅛-inch dowel (Illus. 83b).

After the dowel hole is drilled, saw ⅜ inch off both ends of the block using the rip fence. For smaller boxes ¼-inch will be enough. On the top of the remaining block of wood, draw a circle about ⅜–¼ inch in from the edge of the block leaving extra wood around the dowel hole. This inside circle will be the space inside the canister.

Start the saw cut beside the dowel hole and cut around the inside circle. When the inside block is free glue the entrance kerf closed using web clamps, or a couple of old belts, or anything that will pull the kerf closed without marring the outside surface. It is a good idea to sand the inside walls of the canister a little, before gluing the bottom in place. Once the bottom is in position there is nothing left to do but a little sanding.

Pin the lid to the canister with a short length of dowel. Holding the lid

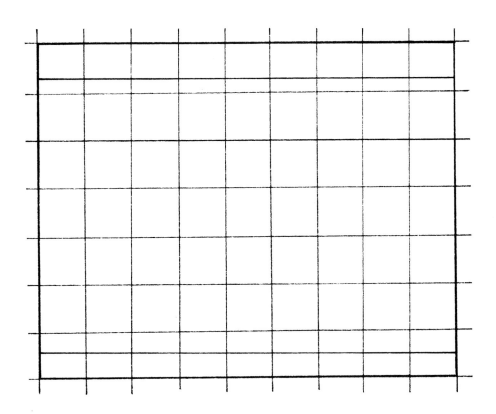

Illus. 83a. This pattern is for a 3½-inch-tall box, but you can make it any size.

firmly in place, sand the outside of the canister either on the belt sander clamped to a bench or by hand. Make sure the lid stays the same size as the canister while you sand.

The finish can be anything you like, or in some cases you may not want a finish at all. If you plan to put food of any sort—candy, nuts, potato chips, etc.—in the canister, you might want to rub it with vegetable oil or a com- mercially prepared oil for cutting boards and salad bowls.

The use you have in mind for the canister will also have some bearing on what type of wood to use. Aro- matic woods tend to impart their aroma to food; cedar smells good but it does not taste good. On the other hand, a cedar canister is great for keeping handkerchiefs, and it will look great on your bureau.

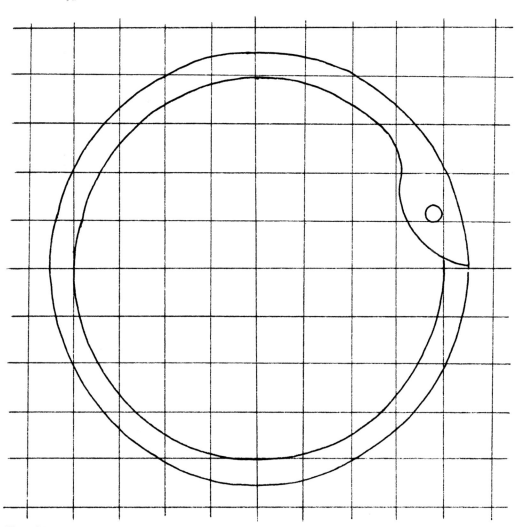

Illus. 83b. The lid of the stump box, with the entrance kerf at right. For canisters under 5 inches in diameter, drill a ³⁄₁₆- or ⅛-inch hole through the lid and into the side of the box. Attach it with a piece of dowel of the same thickness.

Log Box

Illus. 84

There is not much sanding to do on this box. I thought I would mention that first. You could get by without sanding anything at all except for rounding the edges of the drawers. You can leave the saw marks in the face of the box, adding to its rustic look. The box doesn't take much time to make, and you can stack as many as you like in any configuration.

The boxes in the photograph are made from well-seasoned water birch, which is a scrubby little tree that grows along the edges of creeks and drainage ditches everywhere. It has a nice flaky bark that doesn't fall off after the wood has dried.

The tree trunk is about 3½ inches in diameter and cut into 4-inch lengths. Saw ¼ inch off the back, then cut out the drawer block from the front, leaving the side walls about ¼ inch thick. Remove the drawer block and glue the saw kerf shut. Make the drawer by sawing ¼–³⁄₁₆ inch off the front and back, then cut out the

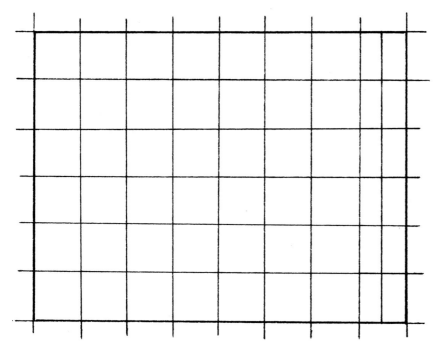

Illus. 85a. The side view of the log box. Saw ¼ inch off the back of the box (right), then cut out the drawer block from the front (left).

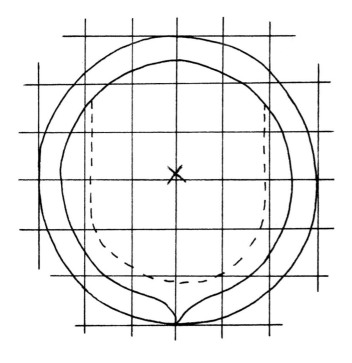

Illus. 85b. The entrance kerf is at the bottom. Cut out the drawer space as indicated by the dotted line. Add a drawer pull at the cross.

drawer space (indicated by the dotted line in Illus. 85b). Glue the front and back in place on the drawer block.

For drawer pulls cut off golf tees about ⅞ inch and glue into a 3/16-inch hole drilled all the way through the drawer face.

The boxes don't need to be finished at all, but I usually spray a little varnish over the bark to help keep out the dust and to give it a little shine.

If you want to stack the log boxes, it's a good idea to glue them together, otherwise when you pull out a drawer the whole stack may come tumbling down. First stack them up and, at the point of contact with another box, sand a flat area along the sides of both boxes. After you do all the boxes in the stack, put a thin line of glue on the flat sides and stack them in the same order and let the glue dry.

Apothecary Jar and Cedar Chalice

The possible variations for this type of box are nearly endless, but the procedure for making them is the same.

The apothecary jar is a piece of 4½-×4-×4-inch light cedar. Do not saw the outside shape first. Saw the inside line, which lets you get right to the hollow part. Cut out the middle by drawing the pattern back on the curved surface (Illus. 87a). Notice that the top of the jar and the widest part at the middle are the same distance from the center line. This is so you can lay the jar on the table with the sides sawn off, if not exactly 90 degrees to the blade, at least close enough.

After the middle is cut out, glue the sides back on the jar. You can begin cutting out the outside shape after the glue dries. There are four sides to

Illus. 86. The cedar chalice (left) and apothecary jar (right).

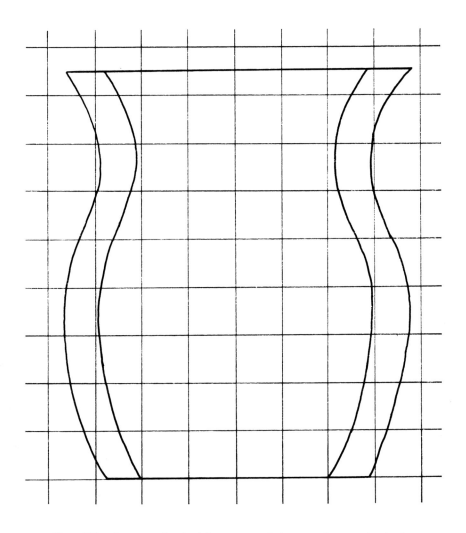

Illus. 87a. Cut out the inside space of the apothecary jar before cutting out the outside shape.

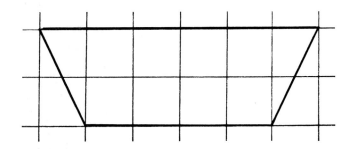

Illus. 87b. The top of the apothecary jar.

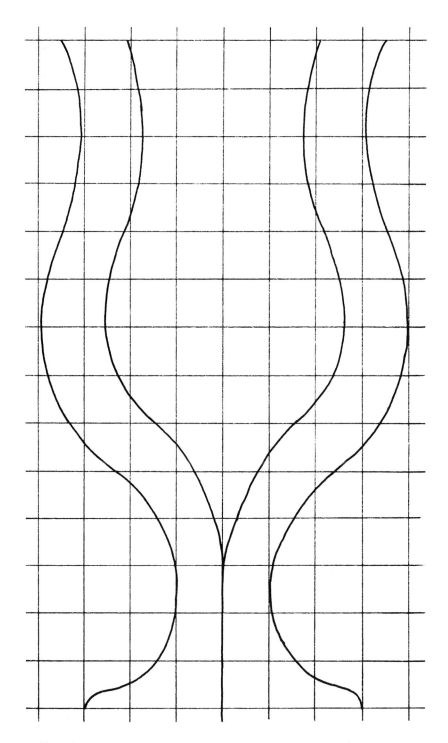

Illus. 88. Cut out the inside space of the cedar chalice before cutting out the outside shape. The saw kerf runs down the middle of the stem.

saw off. Do the first two, then lay them back in place and draw the pattern on one of the sides. With the jar sandwiched between the two pieces cut out the remaining two sides. Use the pattern to make a plug for the top, if you wish (Illus. 87b). Now sand and varnish as desired.

The cedar chalice is made in a similar manner. Cut out the inside lines first (Illus. 88), noticing that the saw kerf runs down the middle of the stem. Cut out the space in the center and glue back the two pieces. Saw the outside shape on two sides and sandwich the chalice between them to saw the other two sides. Now you have a four-sided cup.

To achieve the eight-sided shape, set the saw table at 45 degrees, lay one flat side of the chalice on it, and saw $\frac{3}{8}$ inch off the corner, following the shape of the cup. Taper the saw cutout just below the cup but before you reach the stem, which remains four-sided. If you do this on all four corners, you will have an eight-sided chalice.

Sand the chalice on· the nose of a belt sander; by rotating the chalice as you sand, you can make it round. But only a band-saw boxer can make a faceted shape.

If you wish to make your vessels watertight, coat the inside with epoxy before gluing up and also use epoxy for the actual gluing. This chalice is not to drink out of, mind you, but to hold water for flowers or anything else you'd like to put in it.

Bud Vase

Have you ever noticed that when you put a flower in a bud vase it always leans or falls over to one side no matter what you do? This is not one of the more serious problems of mankind, but it is one for which I can offer a solution.

The vase is made from a piece of wood 2 inches square and 7½ inches long. In this case, I used the limb of an apple tree, which I pruned off last year and left in the garage to dry. Two yellow pine 2 by 4s glued together and squared to 2 inches would also make a nice vase. The holding arm of the vase is a delicate feature and using a softwood will cause it to be even more delicate. However, if the arm ever breaks, the direction of the grain will allow you to glue the arm back in place without ill effects and the arm will be stronger for it.

The first step in making the vase is to saw the shape in profile, then using the rip fence cut ½ inch off each side. Now cut out the space inside the vase indicated by the dotted line in Illus. 90a. This inside space is required to hold water, so it must be sealed and the vase glued with an exterior glue. This is where epoxy is really helpful. Weldwood plastic resin glue is also a good choice. Coat all inside surfaces with the glue as well as the surfaces to be glued together.

After the glue is thoroughly set, cut out the shape of the vase from the front view and drill a ¼-inch hole in

Illus. 89

114

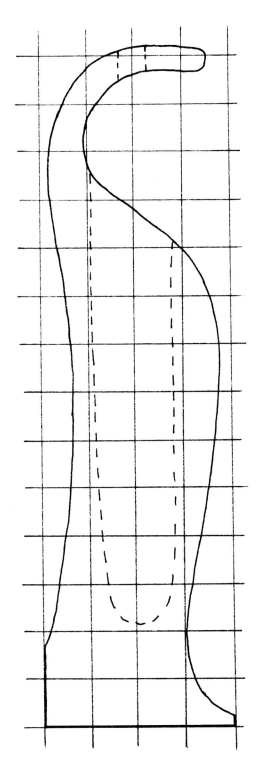

Illus. 90a. Cut out the inside space as indicated by the dotted line in the vase.

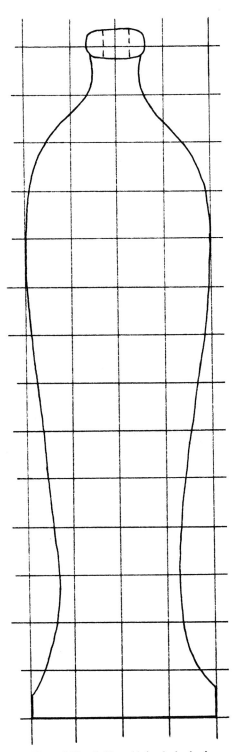

Illus. 90b. Drill a ¼-inch hole in the arm of the vase as shown.

115

the holding arm as shown in the illustration. Now begin the sanding. Always sand the hard part first, which is the underside of the holding arm. This is best done first with a drum sander in your electric drill, then by hand. Shape the rest of the vase on the belt sander clamped to the bench. The shaping involves rounding all the edges until there are no flat surfaces left except at the base. Sand the vase by hand until it is smooth as glass. Give it three or four coats of varnish to protect it from the water, which, from time to time, will be spilled on it.

"A" Box

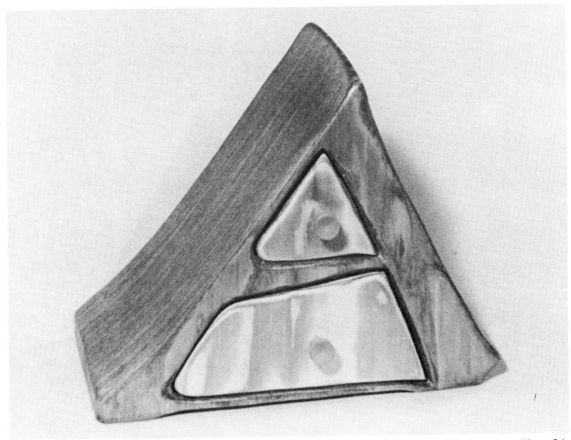

I'm sure this alphabet idea could be extended to include every letter known to man. I'm not suggesting that one person do them all. But, if you had a special need for a given letter, I'm sure you could design a box to meet the need. Designing your own boxes is a lot of fun and there are 25 more letters in the alphabet to serve as inspiration.

This box was made of five layers of ¾-inch plywood 8¼ inches wide and 6½ inches tall glued together. The box doesn't need to be that thick—four layers of plywood would make a nice-size box. Any kind of wood that is big enough would also work well.

Draw the pattern on ¾-inch squares, which is the case in Illus. 92, then transfer to the face of the block of wood. If you are not using plywood, saw ¼ inch off the back of the block. If you are using plywood, you can glue a piece of ¼-inch plywood on the back of the block after the drawers have been cut out.

117

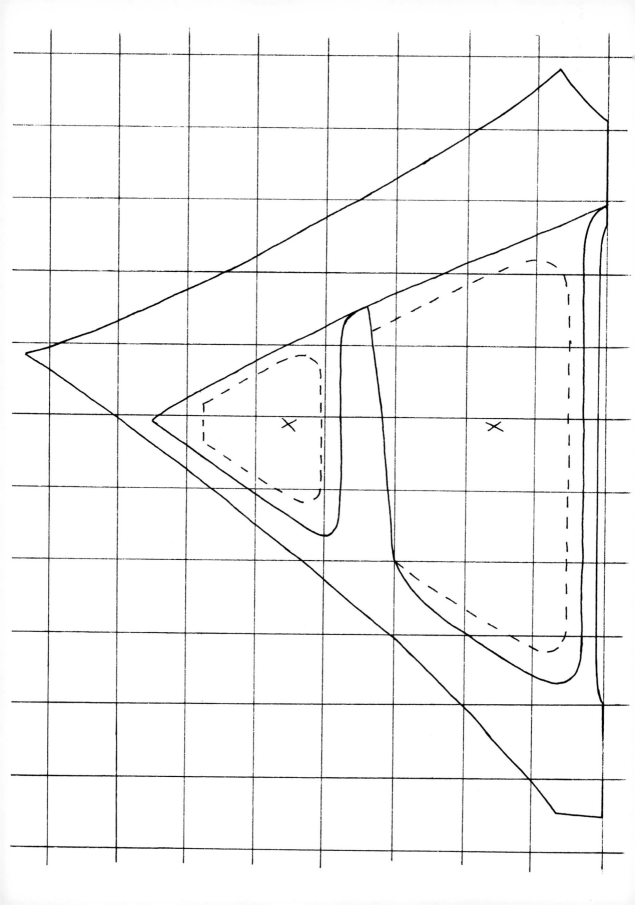

Cut out the drawer blocks from the front using a ⅛-inch blade on the band saw. Start the first cut at the bottom of the right leg and saw straight to the top of the inside of the "A." Back the saw out of the wood and start the second cut along the bottom of the lower drawer. Cut around the drawer and back to the first cut and the drawer block is free. Use the same procedure for the top drawer.

With both drawer blocks free, glue a ⅟₁₆-inch spline in the kerf at the bottom and at the crossbar of the "A." Glue the back onto the block of wood. When the glue has dried cut out the shape of the "A."

Saw ¼ inch off the front and back of both drawer blocks and cut out the drawer space indicated by the dotted line. Glue the front and back on the drawers and add drawer pulls. I used wooden golf tees glued in a ³⁄₁₆-inch drilled hole.

Round all edges of the box and drawers first on the nose of the belt sander, then sand smooth by hand. The "A" part of the box is stained dark and the drawers are left unstained. You could stain the drawers dark and leave the "A" natural with good results. Varnish the box and rub with a little 0000 steel wool and linseed oil.

I hope the "A" box is only a start on your way to "Z."

Illus. 92. Cut out the drawer spaces as indicated by the dotted lines. Use wooden golf tees for drawer pulls at the crosses.

Limb Boxes

There is no sense in giving patterns to follow for these boxes since no two could ever be alike. However, I can at least describe how they are made.

First take the tree limb of your choice and saw it off to the height you want it to be. Get it to stand securely, straight or leaning a little as you wish. Choose the side you want to be the front, which is the side where the drawers will pull out. Now you must saw off the back one third of the limb on the band saw. Keep the piece under control by holding it firmly and moving it slowly through the saw.

With the back sliced off, the limb

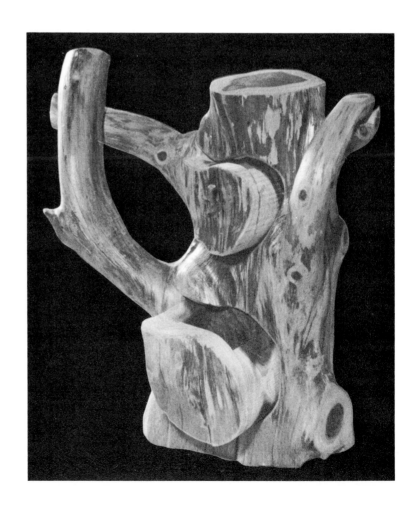

Illus. 93. After sawing off the back one third of the limb, cut out the drawer blocks from the front with separate entrance kerfs for each drawer.

will now lie flat on the saw table. Cut out the drawer blocks from the front. You can make either a separate entrance kerf for each drawer (Illus. 93), or a single entrance kerf for all the drawers (Illus. 94). After the drawer blocks are removed, glue the back on the box.

To make the drawers, saw ¼ inch off the back. Following the curvature of the face of the drawer, saw ¼ inch off the front. Then cut out the drawer space and glue the backs and fronts on the drawers.

It is difficult to clamp irregular shapes. Sometimes it's necessary to cut a "V" shape in a scrap of wood just big enough for the piece to fit into, which gives the clamp a flat footing and applies pressure at the necessary places. Three or four "V" shapes may be required for a single box. Don't throw them away after you use them. If you plan to make other

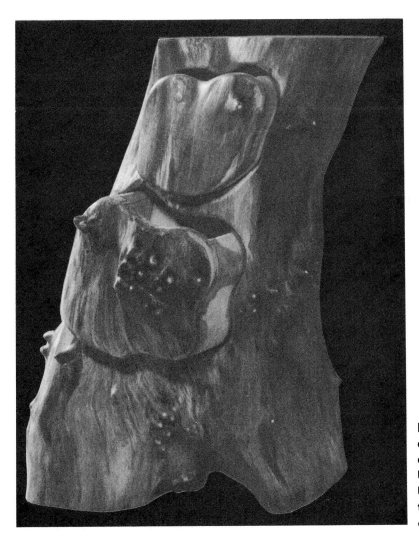

Illus. 94. Cut out both drawer blocks from a single entrance kerf. After the blocks are cut out, glue the back one third of the limb that was previously sawn off.

boxes of this type, they will probably fit them as well.

Drawer pulls for these boxes can be anything imaginable. I usually try to use a natural feature of the wood, such as the knobs sticking out of the large box (Illus. 94). Alternatively, pieces of twig or even bark can be used as drawer pulls.

For the finish, there are about three options. If there is no bark on the box and the surface is smooth, varnish it or rub or dip the whole box into linseed oil, as in Illus. 94. The third possibility (and my personal favorite) is to do nothing at all, which is the case for the limb box in Illus. 93. No two limb boxes will ever be the same.

Metric Conversion Chart

MM—MILLIMETRES   CM—CENTIMETRES

INCHES TO MILLIMETRES AND CENTIMETRES

INCHES	MM	CM	INCHES	CM	INCHES	CM
1/8	3	0.3	9	22.9	30	76.2
1/4	6	0.6	10	25.4	31	78.7
3/8	10	1.0	11	27.9	32	81.3
1/2	13	1.3	12	30.5	33	83.8
5/8	16	1.6	13	33.0	34	86.4
3/4	19	1.9	14	35.6	35	88.9
7/8	22	2.2	15	38.1	36	91.4
1	25	2.5	16	40.6	37	94.0
1¼	32	3.2	17	43.2	38	96.5
1½	38	3.8	18	45.7	39	99.1
1¾	44	4.4	19	48.3	40	101.6
2	51	5.1	20	50.8	41	104.1
2½	64	6.4	21	53.3	42	106.7
3	76	7.6	22	55.9	43	109.2
3½	89	8.9	23	58.4	44	111.8
4	102	10.2	24	61.0	45	114.3
4½	114	11.4	25	63.5	46	116.8
5	127	12.7	26	66.0	47	119.4
6	152	15.2	27	68.6	48	121.9
7	178	17.8	28	71.1	49	124.5
8	203	20.3	29	73.7	50	127.0

YARDS TO METRES

YARDS	METRES	YARDS	METRES	YARDS	METRES	YARDS	METRES	YARDS	METRES
1/8	0.11	2⅛	1.94	4⅛	3.77	6⅛	5.60	8⅛	7.43
1/4	0.23	2¼	2.06	4¼	3.89	6¼	5.72	8¼	7.54
3/8	0.34	2⅜	2.17	4⅜	4.00	6⅜	5.83	8⅜	7.66
1/2	0.46	2½	2.29	4½	4.11	6½	5.94	8½	7.77
5/8	0.57	2⅝	2.40	4⅝	4.23	6⅝	6.06	8⅝	7.89
3/4	0.69	2¾	2.51	4¾	4.34	6¾	6.17	8¾	8.00
7/8	0.80	2⅞	2.63	4⅞	4.46	6⅞	6.29	8⅞	8.12
1	0.91	3	2.74	5	4.57	7	6.40	9	8.23
1⅛	1.03	3⅛	2.86	5⅛	4.69	7⅛	6.52	9⅛	8.34
1¼	1.14	3¼	2.97	5¼	4.80	7¼	6.63	9¼	8.46
1⅜	1.26	3⅜	3.09	5⅜	4.91	7⅜	6.74	9⅜	8.57
1½	1.37	3½	3.20	5½	5.03	7½	6.86	9½	8.69
1⅝	1.49	3⅝	3.31	5⅝	5.14	7⅝	6.97	9⅝	8.80
1¾	1.60	3¾	3.43	5¾	5.26	7¾	7.09	9¾	8.92
1⅞	1.71	3⅞	3.54	5⅞	5.37	7⅞	7.20	9⅞	9.03
2	1.83	4	3.66	6	5.49	8	7.32	10	9.14

Index